WAY OF THE Whitetail

MAGIC AND MYSTERY

WAY OF THE Whitetail

MAGIC AND MYSTERY

Dennis L. Olson

Photography by
Stephen J. Krasemann

NorthWord PRESS

Minnetonka, Minnesota

AUTHOR'S ACKNOWLEDGMENTS

Thanks to Tom Klein for his friendship and companionship during many adventures and for providing the opportunity to do this book. Jack Pichotta, Ken Marienfeld, and my brothers Tom and Ger were there when many of these stories unfolded. Thanks for the enduring company, guys. My Dad first brought deer to my attention when I was young and encouraged my outdoor interests. Mom's wit is found on every page of this text. Thanks also to Douglas Wood, for reinforcing the kind of friendship, creative synergy, and irreverence we both put into our work.

The information in this book represents millions of hours of deer-watching by countless researchers and other fanatics. Thanks to those people for doing most of the work. I hope my version of the story serves you well.

For Jesse and Kya

COWLES
Creative Publishing, Inc.

NorthWord Press
5900 Green Oak Drive
Minnetonka, Minnesota 55343
1-800-328-3895

Designed by Russell S. Kuepper / Calligraphy by Linda P. Hancock

Library of Congress Cataloging-in-Publication Data
Olson, Dennis L.
Way of the whitetail : magic and mystery / by Dennis L. Olson;
photography by Stephen J. Krasemann.
p. cm.
ISBN 1-55971-427-1 : $35.00
1. White-tailed deer. I. Title.
QL737.U55O42 1994
599.73'57--dc20 94-20648 CIP

Printed and bound in Singapore

PHOTOGRAPHER'S ACKNOWLEDGMENTS

This project has allowed me to spenc more time with my friends Tom and Pat Klein, and has allowed me to get to know Russ Kuepper, the designer of this book. Other "deer people" who helped me locate deer around the country include Dan Griggs, Dr. Harry Jacobson, Rusty Dawkins, Ken Carlson, and Steve Heuel.

I would like to extend heartfelt thanks to two people who became "deer" friends over this project and quite frankly, I could not have done this book without their assistance. Stan and Ester Stevenson gave me their time and support for three years and counting. Stan and Ester's love of whitetails is palpable and comes from all their years living with deer.

One last quick thank you is extended to all the white-tailed deer that allowed me to capture one of several moments of their lives for us to relive again and again in this book.

TABLE OF CONTENTS

Introduction
DEEROPHILIA

I remember being too short to see over the dashboard. I was sitting between my Mom and Dad on the front seat, alert. "Deer might be around," my Dad had said. My younger brothers were standing on the back seat, wide-eyed, with their noses barely poking over the bench front seat. Our old station wagon crawled along on the state park road in northern Minnesota, at patrol speed. This was the pre-seat belt era: I kept edging forward so I could see ahead, and Dad kept pushing me back so he could see the road. We rode this way for as long as my five-year-old attention span could hold out.

Eventually we all gave up, of course: my brothers were sleeping down in the cocoon of the back seat when it happened. I had settled far back into the front seat in a daydreaming fog (a state which is, unfortunately, still characteristic). Dad stepped on the brakes and simultaneously, across the arc of the windshield, I saw nothing but red-brown hair, hooves, antlers, and an eye—a dark, calm eye that seemed to say, "We jump over car hoods all the time." Dad smiled his triumphant "I told you so" smile, and I grew up to write about deer.

Siblings, male and female, demonstrate the legendary alertness of whitetails.

The peak of the rut is the only time of the year when bucks are likely to appear along the back roads. This deer is a dominant buck, and, judging by the size of his neck, full of male hormones.

For short distances deer can travel at speeds illegal on most city streets.
They are difficult to cite for speeding, however . . .

I've seen thousands of deer since then, and a small part of every sighting was seen through five-year-old eyes. Deer have been special since then, but only in part because of that early experience. The other part is that deer are special, not just to me, but to a big chunk of the human population.

So, what is so special about white-tailed deer? Grace. Liquid grace. A deer is a visual feast just being a deer, alternately flowing from one spot to another and freezing in place to become part of the surrounding woods. White-tailed deer manifest the kind of grace that makes ballet look almost herky-jerky. I was once an athlete, but my kines-thetic sense disengages when I try to crawl into the figurative skin of a deer.

In addition to their fluid athleticism is an absolute awareness of the world immediately around them. They smell which species is upwind and what attitude it has. They hear every tick of a far-off wristwatch. They zero like a laser on unusual motion, no matter how slight. I swear they can somehow sense a predatory disposition in a human. Their awareness of the "present" would be the envy of any Zen master, but those skills make perfect sense when we consider that they are born to be prey, to pass on their energy to other creatures. They can afford no idle daydreams or memories.

For the deer's own sake, considering their for-midable reproductive potential, it's a good thing they taste good and do substantial crop damage. If it weren't for that, no one but a sociopath would want to kill a deer. They are too darn cute. But like it or not, their role in the natural system can be succinctly defined as "predator food." Their job, harsh as this may sound, is to convert sunlight, in the form of plants, into wolves, cougars, humans, and soil.

A new fawn is more prone to show curiosity than fear.

Defining the appeal of the whitetail is the easy part. The difficulty lies in maintaining at least a relative objectivity about the deer, its world, and its relationship to us.

Don't ask for objectivity from the 14 million American deer hunters, who spend almost 3 billion dollars every year pursuing their pastime. Don't ask the 100 million wildlife watchers, who tell at least 100 million stories about their own deer encounters.

Don't ask me for objectivity, either. Admittedly, my illusions of objectivity about most things have waned over the years, but when I watch deer, the visceral "me" realizes that there are no observers, only participants. It is, I think, clearly impossible for me *not* to arc over a windfall with a deer—as a deer. With that admission I disqualify myself from writing a purely scientific treatise on the whitetail. This is, rather, a book about magic.

But I do have a request. Let your knowledge of deer color your attitudes, not the other way around. Deer are deer. They aren't four-legged humans, nor are they walking bags of venison. The analogies to human life sprinkled throughout this book are just tools to help you understand and remember. If this text says something anthropomorphic (giving human attributes to animals) it is tongue-in-cheek, for humor. I promise

Seeing (foreground) and smelling (background) are two of the whitetail's early warning systems.

to balance the anthropomorphic with some zoopo-morphic comments—giving deer attributes to us. I'll tell you what I, and a few others, know about deer. I might even tell you what I suspect. But I won't lie, at least not intentionally. A quick look at history shows that what we think we know about deer today will turn out to be only half of the story some day. If I'm around, I promise to revise the book.

Secretly, I hope that, after reading my book, at least some of you will drive the back roads a little more often in the hope that a deer will consent to show itself. You will probably see only trees, coulees, and river bottoms most of the time. Be patient. Deer are in there, doing better than they ever have. Just keep your eyes focused, because you never know when one might jump over your car hood and alter the course of your life a little.

There is little "rest" for a whitetail. Alertness is almost constant, even when bedded down.

Chapter One
BEYOND BAMBI

It all started about 20 million years ago, long before we humans dropped to the ground from the safety of trees. *Cervidae*, the deer family, outlasted the mastodons and woolly rhinos and divided themselves into moose, elk, caribou, and *Odocoileus*, the deer. White-tailed deer are found 23 million strong in 48 states and six provinces, so anyone who departs the inner city and watches the woods and fields will see one sooner or later. What *kind* of whitetail they see will depend on where they are.

Science, eternally obsessed with turning black and white into various shades of gray, recognizes 17 subspecies of the species *Odocoileus virginianus*, the prototype Virginia deer. Subspecies will interbreed freely but show obvious geographical differences in their appearance. Even so, the categories are misleading and sometimes almost silly. What do we get when a Dakota whitetail subspecies interbreeds with a boreal whitetail in western Iowa? A sub-subspecies? And if that deer someday mates with a Kansas whitetail?

A newborn is scentless, camouflaged, and usually motionless—until mom arrives. (Note: they are almost never "abandoned," so leave them where you find them.)

A boreal whitetail at the October peak of body weight and aggressiveness is an intimidating sight.

Most plants taste better in the spring when leaves are new. But these milkweeds will contain their foul-tasting milky juice until later in the summer.

Scientists, obsessed with classification, even classify themselves into lumpers (those who tend to minimize geographic and physical differences) and splitters (those who love making subgroups of subgroups). Being a product of the era of political correctness and having a mediation mind set, I tend to emphasize common ground. I am clearly an unapologetic lumper.

I will indulge all the splitters out there by saying a bit about the presently recognized subspecies, emphasis on the word presently. Sure as you are reading this, these groupings will be changed someday.

Don't get me wrong. There are real differences. The boreal (which means northern) whitetail is three times the size of the Florida Key deer, for example. The differences between subgroups tend to be greater with distance from each other or with more geographical isolation.

Five of these subgroups are tiny populations on isolated islands off the Atlantic and Gulf states (Avery Island, Blackbeard Island, Bull's Island, Hilton Head Island, and Hunting Island). Another small subgroup is the endangered Colombian whitetail found only on a refuge near the Columbia River in Washington. I won't dwell on them, but a few of the larger populations have characteristics worth mentioning.

In general, the geographical differences conform to three basic rules of biology. One, the farther north a mammal lives, the larger its body size—usually. A bigger body has more internal volume (furnace) compared to its outside surface area (leaky walls), and is therefore more heat-efficient. The northern woodland whitetail subspecies can weigh up to 350 pounds, and the Florida Key deer tops out at 80.

In southern Texas, prickly pear cactus could be called "protective habitat" for white-tailed deer.

The average weights of adult buck whitetails of the different subspecies are as follows. Keep in mind that does weigh about 60 percent of what a same-aged buck weighs.

Key deer .... 80 lbs
Coues deer .... 100 lbs
Carmen Mountains deer
(Big Bend, TX) .... 120 lbs
Florida coastal deer ...... 140 lbs
Florida whitetail .... 150 lbs
Texas whitetail .... 150 lbs
Virginia whitetail .... 175 lbs
Kansas whitetail
(eastern prairie) .... 200 lbs
Dakota whitetail
(northern prairie) .... 225 lbs
Northwest whitetail
(northern Rockies) .... 225 lbs
Boreal whitetail
(north woods) .... 240 lbs

The range of white-tailed deer weights is broader than these averages would make it seem. For instance, the biggest deer ever recorded was a 511 pound megadeer (live weight) killed in Minnesota back in 1926. An "average" deer, like an average human, is hard to find.

The second rule of thumb is that northern mammals have smaller extremities (ears, tail, etc.) relative to body size. The Coues deer from Arizona and Mexico has ears that cause them to be confused with mule deer. A few years ago, I did a double-take when walking up a creek bed in southeastern Arizona. Standing 20 yards up the hill was a mule deer head on a small, light-colored body with a white tail. It wasn't a mule deer-whitetail cross, just a Coues version of the whitetail. I was accustomed to the other end of the spectrum, having grown up with small-eared Minnesota and Wisconsin deer. The reason for big ears in the hot desert is supremely practical—losing excess heat (by having more surface area) is far more important than keeping it. The opposite is true in the north.

The third general rule is that forest mammals are usually dark in color and animals of the open are light-colored. The Dakota, Kansas, or Texas whitetails of the prairies would look pale in the forested Northwoods or the moist Southeastern woods.

It is worth mentioning that the ranges of these deer also change over time. From 1900 to the 1960s, the Boreal race of deer became even more boreal, expanding its range north far into Canada. The reason for this was the expansion of logging during that time. Deer love new growth areas that follow logging—they are good for deer forage. Since the 1960s, that expansion has reversed itself, and moose and woodland caribou (mature conifer forest dwellers) have moved south into areas where they haven't been since the early 1900s. I bet you can guess the reason.

In the north, the peak of fall color corresponds to the early stages of mating season.

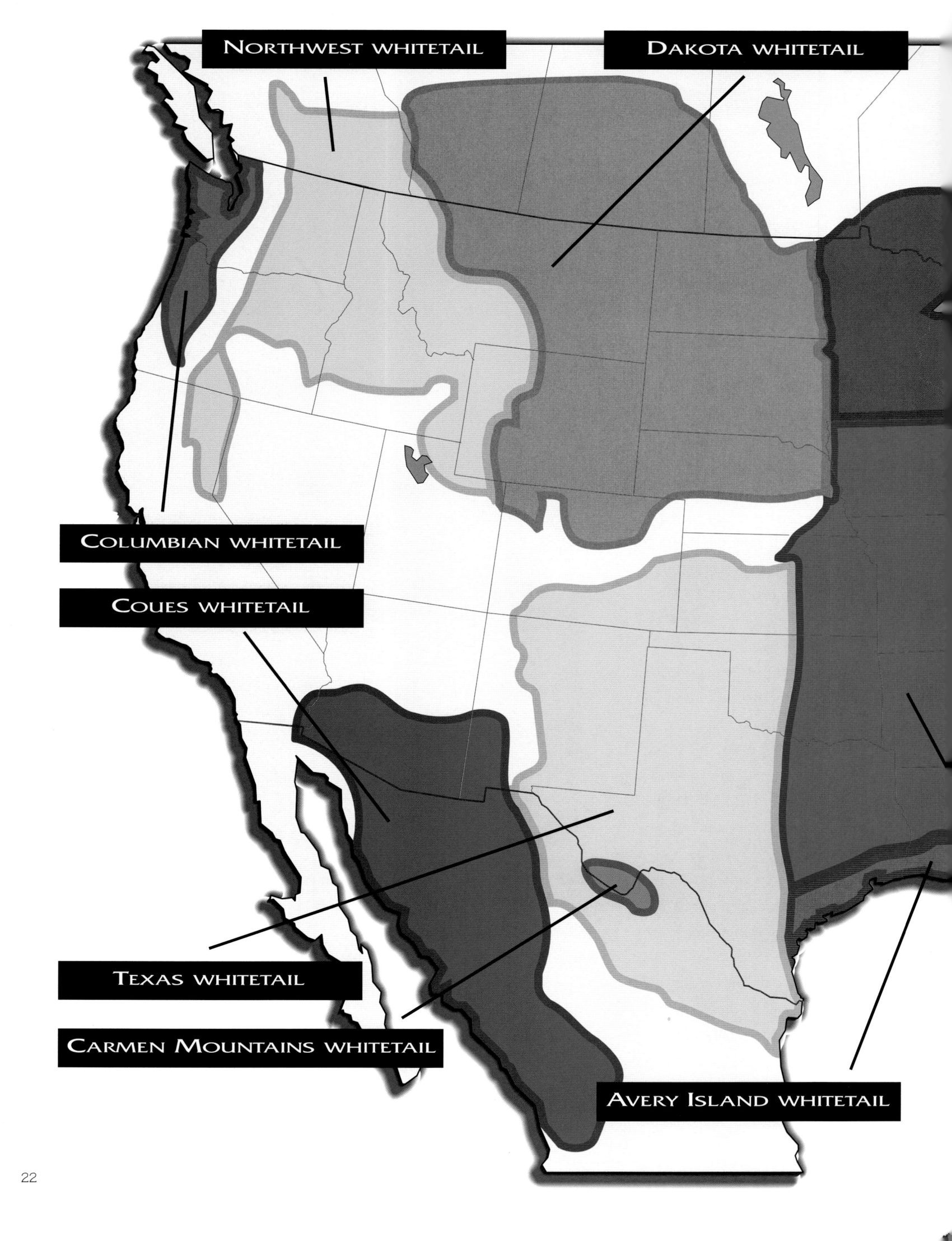

NORTHWEST WHITETAIL

DAKOTA WHITETAIL

COLUMBIAN WHITETAIL

COUES WHITETAIL

TEXAS WHITETAIL

CARMEN MOUNTAINS WHITETAIL

AVERY ISLAND WHITETAIL

22

RANGES OF THE WHITETAIL

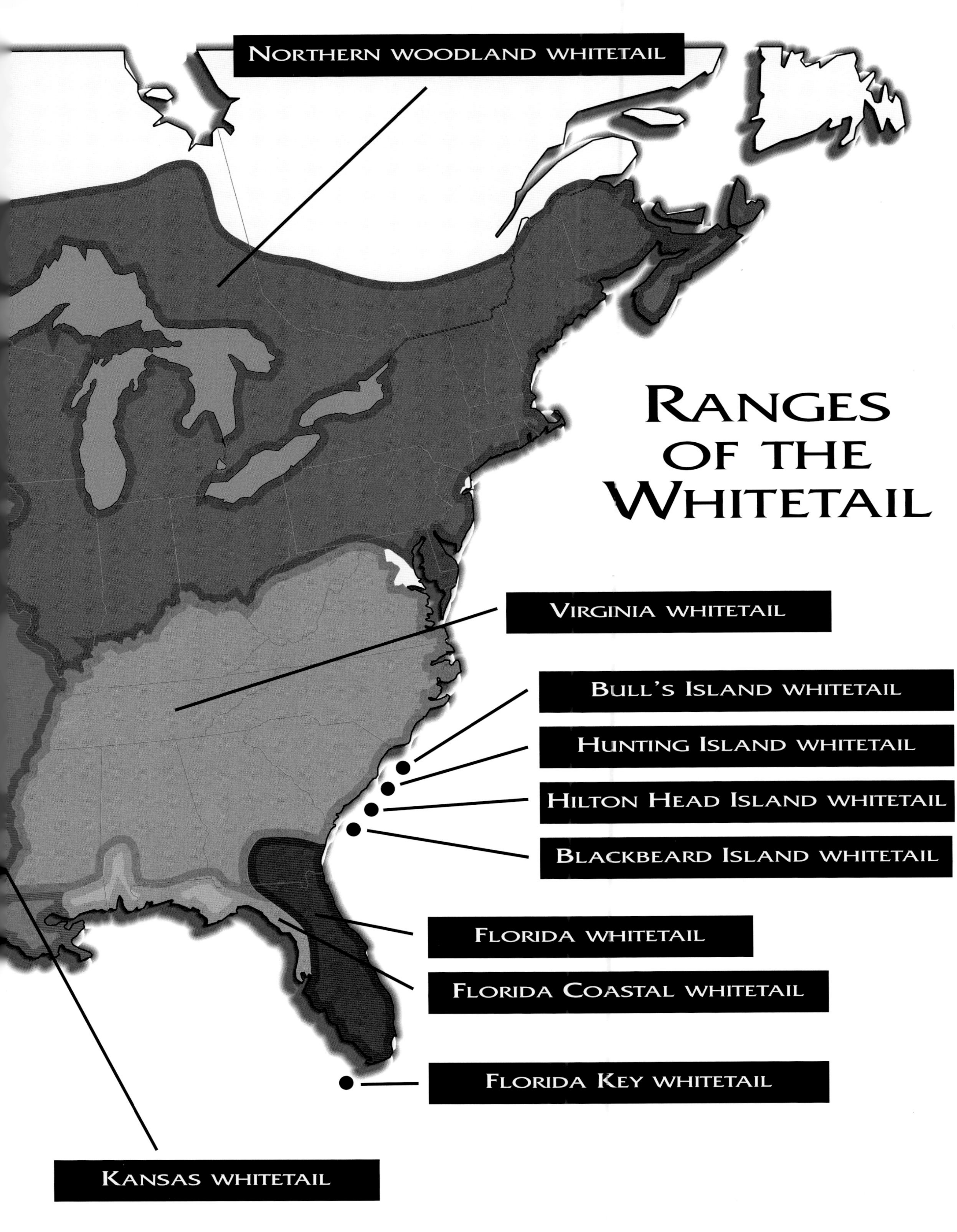

NORTHERN WOODLAND WHITETAIL

VIRGINIA WHITETAIL

BULL'S ISLAND WHITETAIL

HUNTING ISLAND WHITETAIL

HILTON HEAD ISLAND WHITETAIL

BLACKBEARD ISLAND WHITETAIL

FLORIDA WHITETAIL

FLORIDA COASTAL WHITETAIL

FLORIDA KEY WHITETAIL

KANSAS WHITETAIL

Strangely, the behavior of whitetails does not vary much from subspecies to subspecies. The terrain and climate will dictate a few behavioral changes, but from place to place whitetails are essentially whitetails, who would, if placed together, have no problems communicating, mating, or herding .

The physical structure of the whitetail is yet another testament to nature's marvelous adaptations, honed on hardship. The primary survival requirement of a deer, for most of the year, is escape. Deer can run at 40 miles per hour, clear a nine-foot obstacle from a standing position, and bound 20 feet in a zig-zag pattern. That sounds like something rather difficult to catch. In fact, whitetails are nearly impossible to catch if they are healthy and fleeing in their preferred environment. All that leg power comes from millions of years of improvements in design.

Animals that walk most of the time have flat feet, which don't contribute to the length of a running stride. Humans, bears, and raccoons have this type of foot, called "plantigrade" or sole-walking. When nature wanted improvements on the design, along came the cats and dogs (and some dinosaurs), constantly running on their toes. Their foot bones elongated and fused together, which lightened the end of the leg. These "digitigrade" toe-running critters, like the cougar or the wolf, are swift and powerful.

Nature is never complacent or satisfied, of course, so enter the "unguligrade" toenail-running animals, such the deer. The bones of a deer's "foot" are fused into a single slender metatarsal bone, which extends up to the hock, where the hind leg angles forward. This place, almost two feet up from the hoof (or toenail), corresponds to our heel and ankle bones, the tarsal bones. There are no muscles below the tarsal bones, only lightweight and elastic tendons. The fancy term is unguligrade, or hoof-walking. As a whitetail's leg springs backward during a bound, the powerful muscles, high in what looks like the hip of the deer, don't have to move very far. The light bones at the end of the foot move quickly. The result? An agility that a world class athlete would drool over.

Whitetails' long necks serve at least two functions. It gives them great balance when they bound over and through obstacles in the thick woods. It also swivels almost 360 degrees to lock eyes and ears on to potential danger, no matter where it comes from. That smooth circular swing of a deer's head reminds me of the graceful movements of a tai chi martial arts master. If there isn't a set of movements called "the deer," there should be.

Two things about the whitetail's internal physiology are worth mentioning here. First, deer are ruminants, like cows, with four distinct chambers in their stomachs. Time not spent eating is spent chewing what has already been eaten. The eventual breakdown of cellulose wood fiber in the "cud" is a digestive process, foreign to us omnivore types, and is a solid argument against humans being lumped into a purely vegetarian category. Our digestive system says "eat plants and animals" from our teeth at one end to our "scat" at the other.

A whitetail physiological wonder helps them cope with those far-below-zero extremes of the boreal forest. Blood vessels in the deer's extremities— legs, ears, tail, nose—are paired, one artery with one vein. There is a fatty insulation around the pair of vessels. Warm blood, going out via the arteries, warms the cold venous blood coming toward the heart. This ensures that cold returning blood won't shock the heart and lungs. It also ensures that

Velvet-covered antlers, still growing at this point, are relatively flexible and tender.

warm blood won't make it to the ends of the legs and lose vital body heat. The outgoing blood is at refrigerator temperatures by the time it reaches the hoof, but most of the heat has been lost to the returning blood before it can be lost to the frigid atmosphere.

Most of the year, deer are the familiar dull brown color we see on the autumn "big buck" pictures. This hair is long and hollow, present from September to the following May. The dead air spaces in that hair are very efficient insulation. After all, in the northern part of their range, 40 degrees below is not an unusual midwinter temperature.

That hair also serves as a personal flotation device. Twice, in the northern canoe country, I tried to catch a swimming deer in my solo canoe. Both times the deer shifted to overdrive, seemed to rise even higher in the water, and left me behind. And I'm no novice in a canoe. I will be just as amazed the third time it happens, mostly because I still don't believe how fast they can swim. An otter, maybe, but a *deer*?

For a period of time in April and May, the usually sleek deer looks awful. Big patches of winter hair fall out before the winter jacket is replaced by rusty colored short, solid hair—the deer equivalent of shorts and a T-shirt. Deer look positively emaciated in that short coat, and deer-watchers realize how little actual "deer" is in there under all that winter hair.

Deer hair also comes in some more unusual colors. It is not terribly uncommon to see albino (all white with pink eyes), piebald (pinto), or melanistic (black) whitetails. Nature gets bored once in a while, I guess.

Since the critter is called a "whitetail," it would probably make some sense to say something about

Snow melts slowly on the backs of white-tailed deer because hollow winter hair is an effective insulator.

that tail. The long white hairs on the underside of the tail and rump are a flashy and highly effective communication device. Most casual observers know of the tail-straight-up, hairs-erect alarm signal. It's where the whitetail gets its name. There are gradations in the degree of alarm shown by the tail. If a deer is unsure whether there is cause for alarm, but is suspicious, the hair on the rump rises and the tail bobs up and down. Indecision. If the tail rises all the way up but the deer still stands there, it is probably smelling danger but has no idea where the potential predator happens to be. Once a whitetail knows where the intruder is, the "flag" begins to wave back and forth and the deer either heads out with a stiff-legged trot, or, if necessary, a high, bounding run.

The "flag" says a few subtle things, too, which usually aren't recognized by the casual observer. The reason most people don't see them? Deer have to be relaxed and not alarmed for these tail signals to show up. Danger cancels everything else, and the casual observer is usually a potential threat.

Whitetails have a habitual way of moving through the woods. They walk a few steps and stop, straining every sense for a potential threat. Once they have decided all is okay, the "all clear" is given to following deer with a single left-right flick of the

Two fawns, one "flag." These young deer will soon learn to be more decisive about potential danger. Adult deer are seldom ambivalent about a potential predator.

tail. Just one. Then they walk a few more steps and start the process again. This is not altruistic behavior, however. It is much more programmed than that, buried in the genes of every deer. How do I know? Deer flick the "all clear" to no one in particular when they travel alone.

Tails say X-rated things too. Does in heat signal "Why don't you come up and see me sometime?" by holding their tails straight to the side. Bucks signal their intent to comply by holding their tail straight back. Subtle, compared to some postures I've seen in singles bars.

Whitetail communication gets sophisticated, however, when we talk scent. Deer are a walking perfume counter, with different scent glands and different smells for different functions. Since our noses are only about an eighth the size of a deer's, we have to do a lot of guessing about the smells and the functions. The names of the glands (such as preorbital, interdigital, metatarsal) reaffirm Olson's Axiom, which says that the size and complexity of a scientific name is inversely proportional to what we really know about the named object. (Just kidding.)

These are the glands science has identified and the best guesses about glandular functions, starting at the bottom of the deer:

Between the hooves of whitetails is the

Deer are sometimes curious about what another deer is eating. Is the grass really greener by the other deer?

Does in estrous hold their tails half up and to the side. This is the only time of year a buck will get this close.

interdigital (between the digits) gland. A waxy material is secreted from this gland constantly, leaving a scent trail wherever a deer walks. This enables deer to walk exactly where another deer passed as much as two or three hours before. I once watched two Florida whitetails meander across an opening, four hours apart, zig-zagging in exactly the same places.

The metatarsal gland, a white patch on the outside of the lower leg, emits a garlic-like scent into the air when deer are alarmed, according to some observers. From my experience, I know that something in the air warns other deer. I have watched nearby whitetails pick up the cue after the original alarmed deer have left the immediate area. The scent probably hangs around for awhile, because deer who wander into the area an hour later also become alarmed for no discernible reason other than (possibly) the residue from the first deer.

Inside the hock (the angled area on the hind leg of a deer), near a greasy-looking tuft of longer hair, is the tarsal gland. The strong scent of this gland is called a pheromone, which is a fancy word for scents that excite. In the human world, they are a multimillion-dollar business.

There are also anal and vaginal glands whose functions are, for the most part, a mystery to humans. Above the tail is a supracaudal gland. In some species this gland contains oil for water-proofing fur, but again, we humans know very little about its use. The deer know, and that is all that really counts.

In the past, most observers have thought that "buck rubs," places where bucks use their antlers to rub the bark from small trees, were places to release pent-up aggression and perhaps visual signposts to show a buck his own trail in low light.

This is a typical scene from a scrape site. The buck rubs pre-orbital scent on an overhanging branch as part of the freshening sequence.

Conventional wisdom is now expanding to include the probability that scent from the forehead gland is deposited there. Again, reason unknown.

The preorbital (in front of the eye-socket) gland makes a buck's eyes constantly drippy during the mating season. Bucks carefully deposit these drippings on branches overhanging breeding areas.

Considering how important scent is to whitetails, our awareness of these glands and their possible functions is probably only the tip of the glandular iceberg. Perhaps we someday will be able to technically enhance our sense of smell and enter the brave new world of the wolf or deer, or even the migrating salmon. Until then, the best we can hope for is to remain curious outsiders, making moderately educated guesses.

When discussions begin on the physical characteristics of white-tailed deer, the front-and-center subject in the coffee shop happens to be located front-and-center on the deer—at least the male deer.

Antlers. People sometimes call them "horns," but the technically inclined remind the offender that horns stay on an animal and grow constantly, while antlers are shed and are regrown each year. If the technician wants to elaborate further, he or she explains that horns—made of modified hair—put on additional layers each year and are nourished by blood vessels inside the horn. Antlers are true bone covered with a velvety layer while they grow, which feeds the growing antler from the outside.

There is a large mysterious cult in our country, organized around sizes, shapes, and descriptions of deer antlers. "Deer Classics" are conventions where thousands of hunters gather to gawk at hundreds of mounted buck heads. Giant clubs, like Boone and Crockett or Pope and Young, are obsessed with finding ways to quantify the size of antlers for comparison, training officials and publishing huge lists of record-sized antlers from the last hundred years. Nothing, but nothing, about the whitetail can rival the level of human interest in antlers. It's rather ironic that deer actually lose interest every January and toss their own antlers away.

Antler growth is controlled by the pituitary gland, in the center of the brain. The pituitary is controlled by photoperiod, or the length of the day. The shortening days in late summer trigger rapid growth of buck antlers—so rapid, in fact, that there is no faster bone growth known in the animal kingdom (other members of the deer family, like moose and caribou, excepted). This growth takes a tremendous toll on the deer. Scientists who measure these sorts of things speculate that it takes

Antler growth on this deer is nearly complete. Within days the velvet covering will dry and fall off.

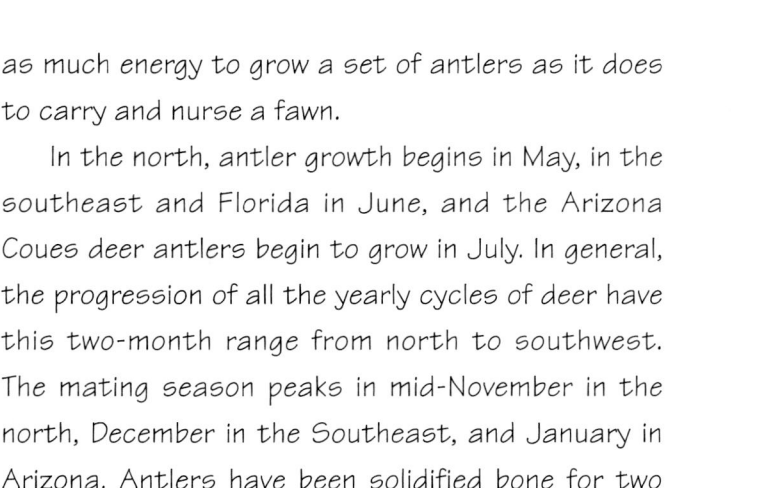

heredity, and nutrition. Bucks have their greatest antler size at five and a half years of age. The antlers usually dwindle in size in the following years. Certain areas of the country seem to have consistently big-racked deer. Often the availability of calcium, phosphorus, and extra protein in the whitetail diet is the critical factor, but certain extended families of deer seem to have the genes for it.

What good are antlers? Seems like a lot of trouble and energy to grow them and carry them around for only half the year. Well, besides being coffee shop conversation, they have uses for bucks. No doubt part of the reason, just like flashing the Rolex and gold chokers, is to impress the other gender. They also are very handy in the pre-rut struggles that establish the dominance hierarchy, or pecking order. Bucks push their antlers together and then attempt to shove each other past the line of scrimmage. The winner mates first, if he is around when a doe is receptive. Contrary to popular misconception, bucks do not have territories which they defend—just rights of first refusal.

as much energy to grow a set of antlers as it does to carry and nurse a fawn.

In the north, antler growth begins in May, in the southeast and Florida in June, and the Arizona Coues deer antlers begin to grow in July. In general, the progression of all the yearly cycles of deer have this two-month range from north to southwest. The mating season peaks in mid-November in the north, December in the Southeast, and January in Arizona. Antlers have been solidified bone for two months by the time the rut peaks in each of those areas, and in general, they are shed two months after the peak.

Antler size is dependent on three things—age,

On one level, antler size matters to deer too. Bucks size up the width of the opponent's antlers carefully before a ritual "fight." If the sizes are very different, both bucks risk being gored in the eye or neck. The obviously smaller buck forfeits the match, and everybody stays healthy.

Chapter Two
TRACK SOUP

Deer. The word is often whispered in urgent and reverent tones by woodspeople. Nothing stops "business as usual" as quickly as a whitetail sighting. And well it should. Despite the fact that over 23 million of them haunt the woods and draws of America (twice as many as only 10 years ago), very few of them are visible at any single moment in time. That shouldn't be surprising. Countless times hunters and/or trained researchers have combed a small fenced area with a known number of deer inside and have spotted only a fraction of them. It's a deer's job to be invisible.

A seasoned hunter expects to be humiliated on a regular basis by the whitetail. Their sensory "toolbox" holds the secrets of their success. Consider their ears, swiveling back and forth, sweeping like submarine sonar. In my most undetectable hiding places, I have seen them move within 15 feet, only to rivet their eyes on my left wrist and bound away. My wristwatch, ticking at a decibel level I can hear at one inch from my ear, was too noisy for a deer at 15 feet.

Even during the distractions of mating season, the first priority is detecting danger.

Whitetail watching rarely involves seeing an entire deer. Usually, you will be looking at a deer who has spotted you long ago.

The so-called "careless, rut-crazed buck" is still the wariest animal in North America.

People hear sounds from 40 to 16,000 oscillations (lowest to highest) per second. Deer hear from 20 to 30,000 oscillations. People have six square inches of reflective ear surface area. Deer have 24 square inches. Aside from all the scientific analysis, some researchers are convinced (with no way to prove it) that deer brains comprehend sound subtleties far better than human brains. They hear smarter.

Part of the sensory mystique can be explained by the whitetail's simple attention to detail. Anything unusual gets their immediate and full attention. A startled jay, crow or squirrel, or even the lack of sound, is enough to ensure a large deer-less radius around an intruder.

Woodspeople and photographers who have been "discovered" at close range have experienced the intensity of a deer's full attention—it is downright unnerving. The deer rivets its eyes and ears on the source of concern, daring the two-legged to twitch or blink or breathe. It may stand like that for 20 minutes while the human listens to its own pounding heart. A favorite trick of the deer is to look away as if it is done examining the suspicious character and then quickly zero back on the human for another five-minute stare. It takes composure to stay calm and still and resist this kind of inquisition. It turns most of us into jello.

The deer's sense of smell is exceptional. The attention they pay to olfactory cues shows that it is by far their most important sense. Something that looks like a human deserves a second look. Something that sounds like a human gets undivided attention for awhile. But something that smells like a human is a human, period.

Deer stalkers go to extremes to avoid detection, usually with frustrating results. Washing body and clothes in soda water, using cover scents that smell like vanilla, skunk, fox urine, various concoctions of deer musk glands, and employing high-tech sprays that "lock" gaseous molecules in place—all get rave reviews from manufacturers and ad agencies and shrugs from veteran wildlife watchers and photographers. Deer are just too good at smelling through the hype.

One of the reasons for the deer's nasal acuity is revealed in a simple measurement. Deer have roughly 100 times the amount of moist surface area in their noses as humans. That doesn't translate to 100 times the smelling power, necessarily. We have as many olfactory cells in our noses as the deer. But most scientists feel (again, without much hard evidence) that deer can differentiate between smells far better than they can discern the intensity of the smell. So, it could be that their brains are better suited for sorting subtle combinations of odors

The "flehmen" posture, upper lip curled back, enhances the sense of smell.

than we can ever imagine. They probably dream in smell, if they dream at all.

Whitetails do two things that enhance their odor perception even further. Bucks have an expression especially during the rut, called the "flehmen," which means that they curl their upper lip back so it touches their nose. Admittedly, I don't know that this posture enhances their olfactory ability, but I have always seen them do it when they stop during an approach toward a mating spot or potentially dangerous area. They "scan" with their eyes and ears at the same time, so I am putting two and two together here.

The second smell enhancer is one with which I have some personal experience. Deer wet their noses, probably to humidify incoming odor molecules and increase the chances of that molecule "locking on" to a receptor cell inside the nose. This technique works for humans too. Next time you are outdoors, wet the outside of your nostrils and sample the air. How many new smells?

I would be hard pressed to add the number of times that I have had deer detect me while they are upwind from me. The nuances of odor—whether it rises, falls, follows eddies in the wind currents, "shears" its way against the wind direction for a few yards—it's all a giant mystery to us small-nosed critters.

Humid air carries more scent molecules, so wetting a nose has a critical purpose.

Another mystery is their ability to accurately "age" an odor. I have often sneaked into the woods and climbed a tree in the hopes of seeing deer, confidant that I would be downwind from their direction of approach. The deer move in and suddenly freeze, looking, smelling, and listening hard. The place this happens is almost always where I have walked. They are smelling my scent trail, not sure

where I am, but knowing that I am somewhere nearby. When I walked on the trail determines what happens next. If it was over three hours ago, the deer will often follow it for a few yards, determine which direction I was moving (I have no idea how), and calmly follow the trail in the opposite direction, moving out of the area in the obvious safe direction. If my trail is between one and three hours old they usually go "on alert," stamping the ground nervously. If the trail is under an hour old, there will be the predictable about-face and exit toward where they came from—the highest-odds safe place.

With my severely limited frame of reference, the only way I can think of the way deer sense odors is to pretend every molecule of every odor is a different color of neon. (Notice that I must use a visual analogy.) That gives me an inkling of what it is like to perceive the world through the nose of a deer. It is clear that I can never really know what it might be like to be in a whitetail argument saying things like, "I don't really smell it that way," or "We just don't smell nose to nose on this issue."

If deer have a weakness in their sensory systems, it is eyesight. Most nocturnal (night active) and crepuscular (dawn and dusk active) animals have retinas (the movie screen at the back of the eyeball) loaded with rod-shaped cells, which gauge

Long eyelashes protect whitetail eyes from twigs as they travel, and the lashes also serve as a handy yardstick to measure the width of openings between trees. This doe could find work as a mascara model . . .

Stamping a foot supplements the visual warning of the tail.

light intensity. We diurnal (daytime) types have retinas packed with cones—color receptors. The result? Deer see well in the dark but are lousy at color charts. We see color vividly, but walk into tree trunks after dark.

Scientists have postulated that deer have a visible light spectrum (like our rainbow) that is shifted slightly from ours. We see red, orange, yellow, green, blue, indigo, and violet—the ROYGBIV we learned in eighth-grade science. Deer probably see a spectrum shifted toward the blues—yellow, green, blue, indigo, violet, and (perhaps) ultraviolet. Somewhere deer adolescents are memorizing YGBIVU for the test.

This skewed spectrum has implications for deer-watchers. At my house, the outside flood lamps over the deer feeders (which also serve as bear and raccoon feeders) are red. The reason? Those nocturnal critters don't realize they are in the light. They don't see red. The other end of the whitetail's visual spectrum has a wavelength of energy, ultraviolet, that is invisible to us. The only way we know it is around is when we peel our sunburned noses. To a deer, however, it is a "color." Brighteners added to laundry detergents enhance the reflective qualities of clothing, making them

Unusual sound or motion is detected simultaneously by every deer in the area—
they know what fits their surroundings and what doesn't.

A whitetail is never far from cover.

slightly "brighter" to us and positively incandescent to a deer. If you want to "blend" irto the woods, be aware that ultraviolet light is real to a deer, but to us is only a pigment of our imagination. Wildlife watchers can wear bright red and not alarm deer, but only under a one condition: They must be motionless. Whiteta Is have eyes that are spaced wide apart, enabling a peripheral vision range approaching 270 degrees (compared to our 180 degrees). Motion is the "red flag" for a ceer, (or more properly a white flag, because that's what we see leaving the scene) and they will always investigate further when a "sturrp" blinks its eyes. Then, one of three things usually happens. If the ccnclusion is "danger," the whitetail will raise its namesake high and be gone. If further investigation is inconclusive, a stiff-legged prance, stomping, and staring will attempt to intimidate the intruder into further movement. If all is clear, the deer will flick its tail once and go about its business. This flip of the tail is the only good sign that the deer is relaxing its vigilance—until the next unusual stimulus.

Over years of evolution accelerated by hunting, deer have learned to be suspicious of a "stump" that is more or less six feet tall and has a small knob at the top. Even when motionless, the human silhouette raises the hair on a deer's neck. So, when

Predators often pass within a few feet of a whitetail. Deer will watch carefully for evidence they have been discovered (such as eye contact). If they feel they can get away with it, they will stay hidden.

No matter where whitetails live, thick cover is always near. The brush
country of Texas is some of the thickest.

deer-watching, use the background to break up your telltale outline. A big tree trunk works well.

In summary, the keys to getting inside a deer's defenses are no smell, no sound, no motion, and no silhouette. In other words, the only thing that always works is to be dead and hermetically sealed in odorless plastic. If we want to watch wild deer close up, the best we can hope for is to get lucky.

That's what we know about the senses of a deer. The fascinating story, at least to me, is what we don't know. How does a whitetail know to flee from a hunter or hungry wolf when it is still a quarter mile away and then graze unconcerned 50 yards from a farmer or a wolf just passing by? The new-ager would say it's ESP. The scientist would attribute it to some subtle cue that we don't recognize and call it "instinct." These are all euphemisms for "who knows?" There is a lot of mystery in this world, and deer perception defies easy and logical explanations. For the time being, it might even be called magic. I like that. If there is anything humans are short of, it is humility. Deer supply it for us in abundance.

All of the whitetail groups have one behavioral thing in common. They love cover, the thicker the better. To a point. The ability to flee quickly from cover is critical, so the brush can't be too thick to prevent easy escape. The other component of deer cover seems to be a good vantage point, especially on the downwind side.

Brush piles, brambles, windfalls, and briar patches are the habitat of choice, especially when resting. Of course that preference is completely logical: any predator of deer will sound like a truck coming through that kind of stuff. To maximize the difficulty of a predator's approach, deer often bed in the woods in sight of an opening, with the wind at

their backs. Thick, noisy cover on either side completes a security system any bank would envy.

Deer also have a tendency to travel on trails recently used by other deer. If one deer made it through the area on that trail just an hour ago, it is usually a safe place to travel. Again, natural selection at work, and working, to human minds at least, very logically. Deer travel on trails, but that doesn't make them very predictable. They usually have many trails coming to a feeding area, and, as far as I can tell, they use them randomly. I have tried in vain to find some correlation between weather, moon phase, time of year, wind direction—and the trail on which they emerge from the woods. It's roulette, and the odds favor the deer.

Whitetails prefer dawn and dusk for their movements to open areas. Some deer become active at a certain time of day and a predictable intensity of light, almost to the minute. Deer probably feel safest in changing light because likely predators, especially two-legged ones, have difficulty making the adjustment. It takes our eyes about an hour to adjust completely to the dark. I would guess that deer do it much faster.

All of these sensory and behavioral traits of whitetails translate to elusiveness. They are very difficult to see, let alone catch. It's why they

Deer blend into the forest at any time of the year. Whitetail watchers should look for horizontal lines in the vertical background.

Openings create a dilemma for deer. The best food grows in the most dangerous places.

thrive, even in our rapidly changing world. Even the best deer watchers often sit motionless for a week, totally camouflaged and cover scented, high in a tree, just to brag that they "saw one" today, barely, at a hundred yards. Hunters have a name for the typical rewards of a day afield in search of deer. It's called "track soup."

Of course we value intellect as the trait of "higher" animals. Deer are long on instinct and short on our version of logic. They are rather stupid, compared to us and our computers, satellites and complicated business deals. But, if just once we could let deer design an IQ test, the first question might be, "Which odors on the wind right now are edible, which are dangerous and which are neutral?" Who flunks that test? Perhaps it is easy for us to perch at the top of the evolutionary ladder when we make the rules.

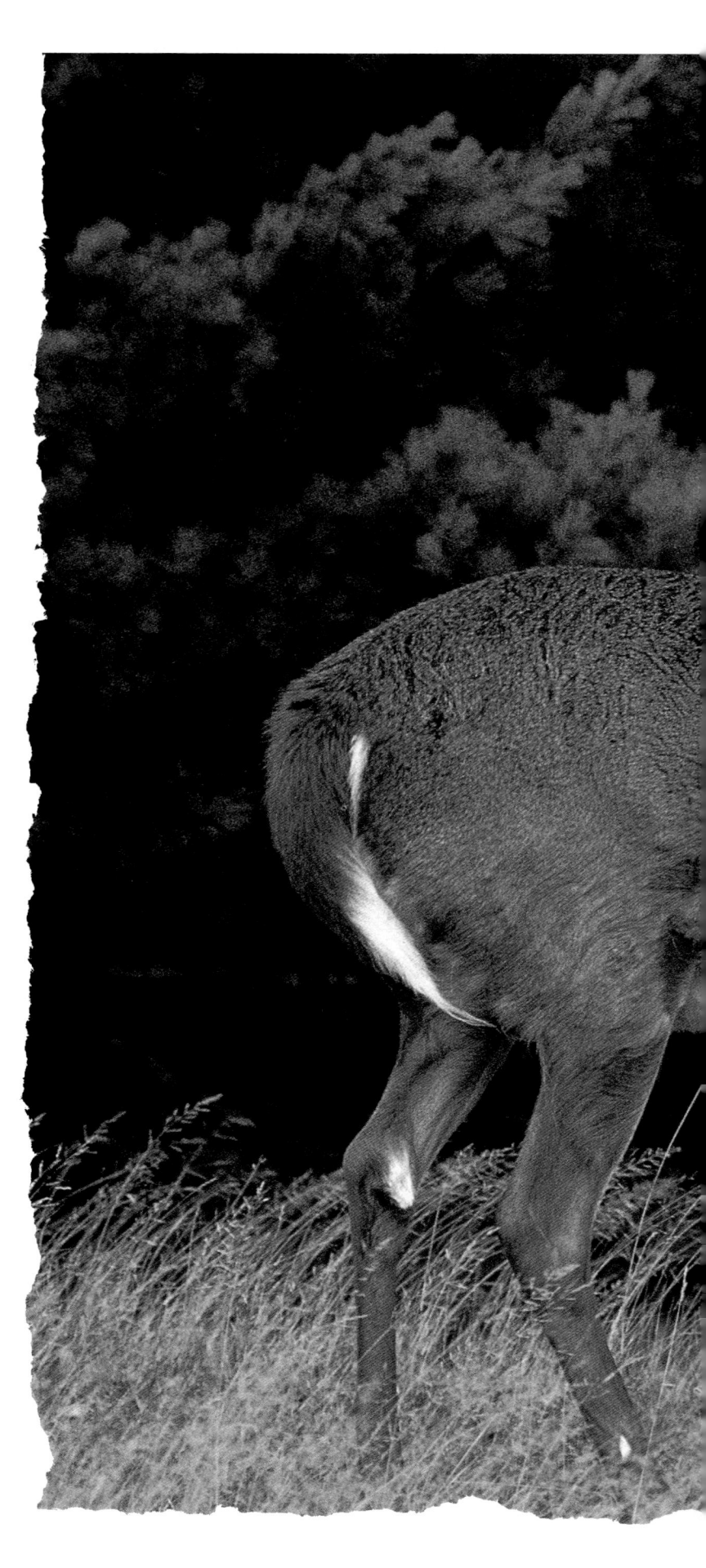

White-tailed bucks often "hide" their white tail— if they think they can escape undetected.

Chapter Three
EVIDENCE

What we usually see of deer is what they leave behind. Evidence. Signs. These leavings can transform into fascinating stories with some careful observation. Tracks tell tales.

Deer are cloven-hoofed animals, which means that each hoof is divided down the centerline. The hoof material is keratin, the same material as fingernails and toenails. Farther back on the leg are the dew-claws, two small evolutionary remnant knobs. They are the modified toenails of two other "toes." The dew-claws don't show up as tracks until deer walk in snow or mud.

Deer hooves grow constantly but the natural wear of walking cancels the growth. The hooves of swamp country deer are longer because the soft soil doesn't wear them back as quickly. In general, the sizes of autumn deer tracks, from tip to dew claw, range from three and a half inches for fawns to six inches for the largest bucks. Buck tracks are slightly more rounded at the tip than doe tracks, but on the front hooves only. Since deer are "perfect walkers" (rear hooves fit exactly into the front tracks during normal walking),

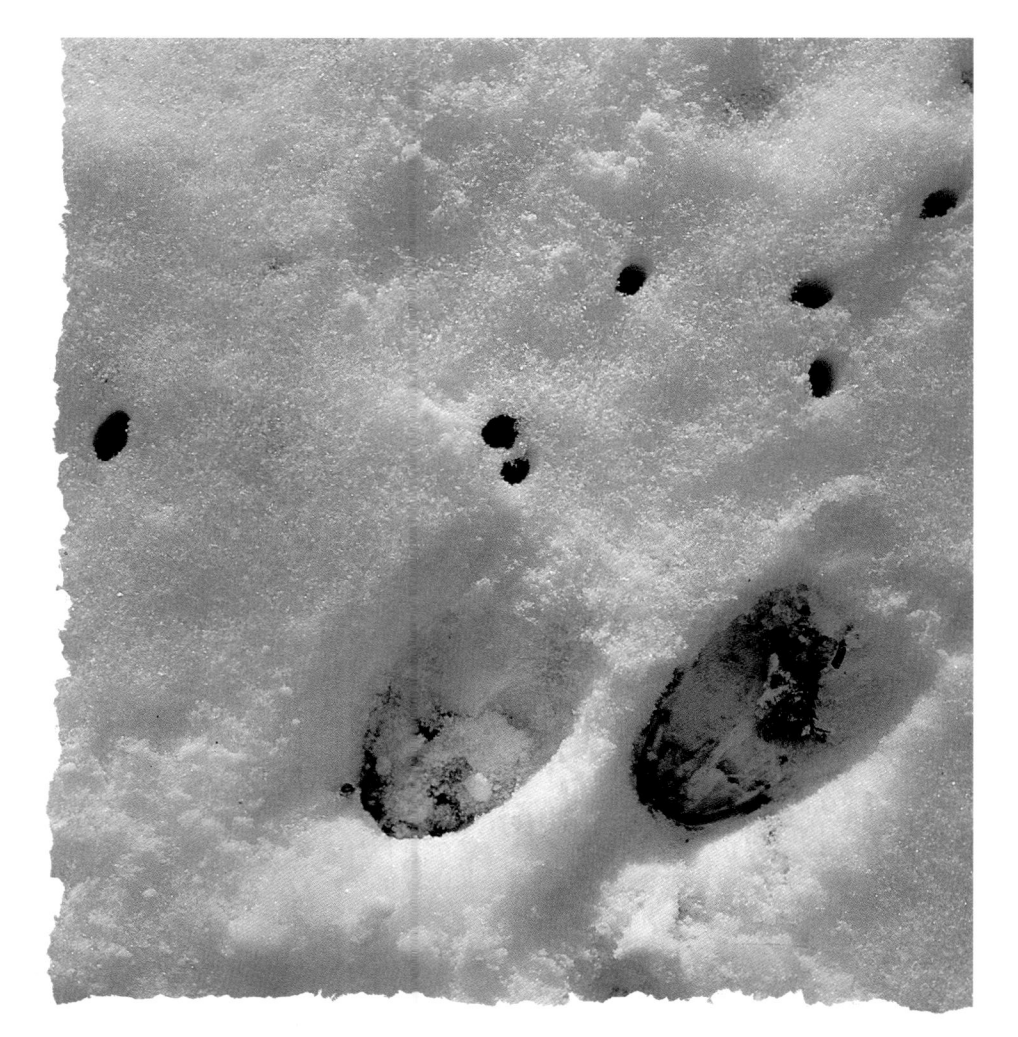

Fresh snow makes deer evidence obvious.

Antler-rubbing releases excess energy, deposits forehead scent, and makes visual signposts for other bucks.

New snow can also erase evidence.

this rounded-toe characteristic is invisible until the deer does something other than walk. Another buck habit is foot-dragging, which shows up in three to six inches of snow. The closer to the peak of the mating season, the more exaggerated the foot-dragging gets. I'm not sure if bucks are just worn out from all the action or there is some other physiological or behavioral reason. Anthropomorphic human interpretations of this trait range from a "swagger" to "typical lazy male" to "just showing off." Adult doe tracks are usually around four and a half inches. A leg injury can cause a whitetail's front and rear tracks to be slightly offset, so that two tracks show instead of one.

The tracks of a secure-feeling whitetail are evenly spaced—one foot in front of the other. If the deer is feeding, the ambling tracks will meander back and forth to food sources. A mildly alarmed deer will trot away, reflected in the gait as a greater distance between the ambling tracks. An emergency escape demands that whitetails put distance between themselves and the danger. Tracks of an escaping deer are clumps of all four tracks spaced 15 to 25 feet apart.

Tracks can also be aged in snow—assuming temperatures below freezing. If the track edges are still soft, the track is probably less than an hour old. If it has an ice crust around the upper edge, but the bottom is still soft, it is probably one to four hours old. Tracks older than that are frozen in the bottom, too. (Keep in mind that bitterly cold temperatures shorten these times considerably.) When the sun shines on these winter tracks, it melts them outward, enlarging the track. Be careful about judging size on those days. A doe track looks like mega-buck after a couple of days of melting.

Lots of tracks, of course, make a trail, and

Browsed twigs appear "ripped" by deer and "snipped" by other animals.

intersections are good places to watch for deer. Trails lead, in general, from bedding areas to food. Beds, usually placed in the most unapproachable places available, look like egg-shaped depressions in the forest leaf-litter or snow. They average three feet long for fawns, about three-and-a-half feet for does and four-and-a-half feet for larger bucks. These larger buck beds are usually found by themselves (does and fawns move together in extended matriarchal family units) and next to an impenetrable swamp or bog, for easy escape.

Deer eat twigs and buds (definitely a high-fiber diet) during the winter, and browse sign is easy to spot. Since whitetails lack upper front teeth, they must rip the tips of branches, leaving a ragged end on the twig. Other browsers, like beavers, porcupines, or rabbits, snip twigs cleanly, and leave a neatly sliced, angled tip. In the summer, deer are grazers, eating a wide variety of grasses, clover, and leaves. An easy way to remember the difference is to be alliterative about it—browse, brown, branches and graze, green, grasses.

Favorite foods are very seasonal and deer will migrate many miles, in some cases, to a temporary source of those foods. Acorns are a classic example. Corn, alfalfa, cedar, aspen, dogwood, mountain maple, ash saplings, hazel—they are all good

The best evidence of a deer is—a deer . . .

whitetail foods. Considering the range of the white-tailed deer, there are probably thousands of kinds of deer food in North America.

What goes in, of course, must come out. Deer droppings, or scats, are different seasonally. During browsing times (fall, winter, early spring) they resemble coffee beans, but in summer they mash together (softer foods) and form one chunk. Budding "scatologists" might feel compelled to analyze droppings further, with a magnifying glass, for specific food types. Be prepared to get some "scat" from your friends, however, if they find out what you are doing.

Droppings can tell us a few other things with some careful observation. Fresh droppings are warm and shiny. Cool and shiny droppings are less than a half-day old. Older droppings are dull. Winter scats can also give us a who's who. For some reason, bucks are more anal-retentive about their excretory functions. They are neater. Buck droppings are usually found in a compact clump, and their urine marks are a small hole in the snow. Does tend to stay on the move during these activities and spread it around a bit.

After bucks shed their velvet antler-coverings in early September (October or November farther south), they begin to succumb to a malady familiar to anyone who has raised adolescent boys. Testosterone poisoning. Physically, bucks put on muscle weight, begin to produce sperm, and get more than a little frisky. Since they don't have high school football as an option, whitetails must find another outlet for their pre-mating frustrations. Small trees are handy almost everywhere in deer country, and they offer varying resistance, depending on their size. When bucks "polish" their antlers by rubbing trees, they say a variety of things both to themselves and other bucks.

In early September, bucks often help the velvet shedding process along by rubbing their antlers on flexible saplings. Later, in October, according to some observers, they announce a breeding range with rubs along their regular routes. Buck trails are often used by a single buck, and it is possible to stand next to a rub and, with careful observation, see the next rub up the trail. Bucks may use them this way as beacons in low light. Near the bedding area of a buck, the rubs are usually clustered, which probably reflects some restlessness while waiting for the sun to go down. I watched a Missouri buck rub, bite, and rip all the vegetation within reach. At first I thought perhaps they just made them meaner in the "show me" state, but then I watched as a nearby doe materialized, followed by a smaller buck. The big guy ran him off.

Some people think that the size of the rubbed tree, which can be up to six inches in diameter, indicates the size of the buck. Sounds logical, but I have yet to see a big tree being rubbed, so I plead ignorance. I have watched huge bucks rub on very small saplings, however.

In the north, bucks begin making ground scrapes in mid-October, and as with other mating-related activities, they start a month later in the Southeast and two months later in the desert Southwest. They paw the earth bare with their front hooves, usually under an overhanging branch near an intersection of doe trails. The dominant buck in the area chases away lesser bucks and patrols up to 50 of these scrapes once every day or two, sometimes "freshening" the scrape with scent and sometimes passing 50 yards downwind to check it with his nose. The reason these scrapes are made has to do with the logistics of the dating game.

Freshly-discarded antler velvet quickly dries and shrivels. Finding it later is very difficult.

Does in the north come into estrus, ready to mate, in mid-November (December in the Southeast and January in Southwest). This "in heat" time lasts only about 24 hours—the rest of the time does are saying "Thanks, but I'm already involved in a meaningless relationship" or "I only date my own species" or some such rejection. Needless to say, it is imperative to a buck to be able to find the doe *du jour* during that day, or vice-versa. Enter the singles bar, the scrape. If a buck is regularly freshening a scrape, every day, all a doe needs to do is wait near the scrape until Mr. Right arrives. The catch here is that almost all mature does come into heat in just a few days. That means dominant bucks are getting exhausted and subordinate bucks are sneaking in to catch the indiscriminate does when they are vulnerable. It is a crazy few days.

Bucks begin freshening scrapes by licking and biting the overhanging branch and depositing preorbital scent on the branch. Then they paw an area clean under the branch, ranging from a foot to 10 feet in diameter (macho buck or overkill when they get that big). Next they step into the scrape and deposit some tarsal gland scent (Brut or Calvin Klein) into the fresh earth of the scrape. Tarsal scent is not very liquid, so the buck rubs his tarsal glands together, hunches his back, and urinates over his hind legs, washing the scent into the scrape. Sound romantic?

Interestingly, the does often decide which scrapes get a lot of buck attention by doing the same pee-on-my-legs routine as the buck. As tricky and intense as it sounds, this method certainly works. Every year many millions of fawns are born in the woods of North America. If the routine sounds strange, imagine what an objective deer might

"Freshening," a scrape is done by urinating over tarsal glands, washing scent into the bare earth.

observe in a human singles bar. Scary thought.

The "singles bar" analogy is not without its skeptics. Ken Nordberg, as professional as a deer-watcher gets, is convinced that scrapes have more to do with bucks talking to other bucks (a la corporate maneuvering for the corner office) than they do with attracting does. Only the deer know for sure.

In June, a delightful deer sign is the "delivery room," where a female has given birth. Look for a small area five or 10 feet in diameter where the ground vegetation has been tidily cropped. This is where the new mother ate all of the fluid-stained vegetation to erase the scent of a vulnerable newborn. (Should you ever discover a fawn, don't assume it is "abandoned." Leave immediately, so the mother can come back and attend to her duties.)

Whitetail sounds are another good sign of a deer in the immediate vicinity. (How's that for understatement?) Whitetails communicate by sound more than their usual silence would imply, and the sounds fall into four basic categories. Larry Marchinton and crew in Georgia have identified 12 separate nuances of the basic four.

Family communication, usually between does and fawns, consists of bleats, which sound like sheep-bleats without the quaver in the voice.

A large rubbed tree usually (but not always) means it was rubbed by a large buck.

This buck has fresh bark on its antlers from rubbing a tree.

They probably signal distress and the whereabouts of deer who can't see each other.

Snorts scare the bejeesus out of people walking in the woods at night. They sound like the sudden release of steam pressure from a boiler. The message is, "I see you. I'm suspicious. If you are a potential predator, you've been had." I jump every time I hear it, even when I know it's coming.

Bucks "grunt," a sort of short muffled belch, when they are on the trail of a doe in heat. It could be a pick-up line, something like, "Hi baby, what's your sign?" A "snort-wheeze," which sounds like a rapid-fire repeated inhale-exhale, is used in a competitive situation, primarily between challenging bucks.

Sleuthing the stories of deer by tracking and watching for their signs is addictive, definitely a lifetime sport. After years of detective work, expect to think like a deer. Every once in a while, when I'm on the trail of a deer, I catch myself testing the wind.

Open woods such as these are fairly typical bedding sites. Whitetails like to lie down at or near the crest of hills, both for visibility and a hidden escape route down the far side of the hill.

Chapter Four
DAY OF THE DEER

First, there is no "typical" day of a deer. From everything I see, whitetails simply exist to eat and evade predators. Food is seasonal and dependent on location, weather, and competition. Predators use unpredictability as one of their primary tools. This makes identifying a "typical" day a practical impossibility. It's like trying to describe an "average" day of fishing—the great days get watered down and the slow days get exaggerated—and the day described as "average" never actually happened.

So, this chapter won't be a typical, average, par, mean, standard, normal, or median day. It will only be a day in the life of a deer.

As you will see in the following chapter, a winter day for a buck is radically different from a spring day for a doe, or a fall day for both genders. I was curious what happens to a deer during a 24-hour period, but I had to decide when to do it. Fall is too crazy with mating and hunting seasons to do a 24-hour day-watch. Winter is too cold for wimpy observers like me to be perfectly still. Spring and early summer have too many bloodthirsty little vampires for my tastes. So, if it appears that I

New fawns are often left for hours by their mothers, with good reason. More visits means more scent left behind by the adult deer, increasing the fawn's chances of being discovered.

Sightings of deer in the early morning and late evening have led to a mistaken belief that deer are only active at those times. Activity cycles continue throughout the day and night, but whitetails are more likely to be in the open at dawn and dusk.

Dominance is decided the old fashion way, with ears back and hooves flailing.

couldn't cut it as a deer during most of the year, even for a day, your perceptions would be correct. Give me a nice, mild August day, thank you.

I also must make two confessions. Being a clumsy *Homo sapiens*, I am unlikely to get near whitetails for more than a few minutes at a time in the wild. I was forced to cheat: The deer I watched were in an enclosure. Even though the whitetails in the enclosure were not likely to encounter predators, they still behaved as if wolves, cougars, and bears were everywhere.

Even with 40 acres the maximum extent of their wanderings, I lost them once in a while. Lucky for me, this kind of observation had been done before. To fill in the blanks, I depended on some observations of hand-raised deer by scientists at the North Central Forest Experiment Station near Ely, Minnesota.

In the wild, white-tailed does have a home range of about one square mile. At this time of the year (August), deer often loosely associate in matriarchal groups of two to six. Groups of antlered deer sometimes affiliate in the same way. In the female-and-descendants groups, there is usually a strict order of dominance based on experience. The dominant deer almost always travels first in line, with fawns and lesser does behind. If there is a particularly tasty food source, she also eats first and defends the food aggressively.

The amount of wariness in a deer is primarily dependent on age—it is learned behavior. I picked a relatively tame older doe to watch for the 24-hour period. Her two, mostly grown fawns stuck with her nearly all the time, but she called most of the shots, initiating travel, feeding, and alert postures for her offspring.

Science would have me recount the events of

Like other species, including some humans, fawns are born with blue eyes which later turn brown.

the day as an "objective" observer, and indeed, I tried to maintain some intellectual and physical distance from this deer and her fawns. Because of this I probably should have labeled her "Adult Female 1A" or some such quantitative classification. On the other hand, I am aware that observation is just another form of participation—the full consequences of which are almost never immediate or apparent. With this in mind, I *could* have abandoned all objectivity and waxed eloquent about Dorene the Deer and her two fawns, Fiona and Fred. Instead I settled for "D" and "F&F" as a compromise.

I began my watch at first light.

5:05 am: D and Company, in fine American tradition, were eating apples. F&F rolled and chewed those on the ground, but D preferred fresher produce—she stood high on her hind legs and pulled apples down. They spent about two-thirds of their time watching and listening intently, the other third eating. This seemed like an inordinate amount of time devoted to evading predators, but as I was to discover, this ratio was relatively relaxed for them. As the sky lightened in the east, they seemed to feel less and less comfortable in the open and spent about nine-tenths of their time on "yellow alert." This seemed extreme by human standards, but paranoia is only paranoia when there is no reason to be jumpy. Whitetails have more reasons to be careful than almost any animal in North America.

5:50 am: Sun up. D looked to the east and stared motionless for four minutes, finally taking two "stomp-steps" toward whatever it was (I heard nothing). The male fawn raised his tail halfway, back down, and then slowly to full upright position. The tail "glowed" with fully erect white hairs from the bottom of the rump to the tail tip. Hard to miss. The fawn then trotted slow-motion and stiff-legged toward the woods, waving his flag in time to the slow trot. It looked half-hearted and it was. He stopped after 75 feet and turned to look at D—just to see if the show was warranted. She was still looking at the same spot. D finally flipped her tail once in the "all-clear" manner, and he immediately turned and walked back toward the apples.

I have often watched groups of deer spiral their various stages of alert out of control, one deer starting with a stomp or a snort and each successive deer reacting more strongly than the preceding one until they all bound away, escaping the nonexistent predator. Often the dominant doe is the last to go, trusting herself more than the others, but still, reluctantly, taking no chances. I can almost see her rolling her eyes and saying, "Here we go again . . ."

Fawns have over three hundred spots in their camouflage patterns.

6:55 am: The three deer fed as they moved, and as they came closer to a small knoll next to another swamp, they slowed their forward progress and fed more than they walked. The general direction of travel was erratic, almost in circles. Finally, D lay down, front legs folding and then her stern following the bow to the ground. Within a minute, the fawns did the same, each deer about 30 feet from the other and facing in three different directions.

They spent 20 minutes watching, swiveling their heads 360 degrees, swiveling their ears when their heads were still, and testing the air with noses stretched high every few minutes. Finally they relaxed and began to chew their cuds, still watching intently but not moving their ears as much or test-

Does recognize their fawns by scent.

6:15 am: D finally began to move west toward the woods. She stopped and took a few nibbles of the short grass by the edge and then stepped in. F&F fell in behind, single file, nose to tail. They moved on the high ground around the edge of a large open marsh, stopping to nibble occasionally. They moved through a narrows between the marsh and an adjacent hay field, staying in the moderate cover but avoiding the thick alders by the edge of the marsh and also moving around the edge of a stand of two-inch diameter aspen saplings. They avoided the densest cover during the entire day, unlike some mature bucks I have watched who were consistently living in the thickest brush imaginable.

ing the air as obviously. It seemed as though the chewing was loud enough to inhibit hearing, because they would always stop chewing to listen when some motion in the distance alerted them.

Gradually, after another 15 minutes of chewing and watching, their eyes half closed and they became (for deer) very relaxed. The fawns eventually lay down their heads and fell asleep for about three minutes. D didn't sleep during this rest cycle.

8:08 am: D rose, defecated, urinated, and began to eat hazel and mountain maple leaves within 10 feet of her bed. Again, the fawns took their cue from D and rose to feed. They covered 200 feet in an hour, moving north along the edge of

Chewing cud is noisy and makes seeing potential danger more important.

the swamp. On another knoll they again lay down, spent a period at full alert, a period chewing, and a tiny amount of time sleeping. D did indulge this time, for two minutes.

When these deer were not interrupted, this feed, move, bed-at-alert, chew, and rest cycle continued throughout the 24-hour period. The only difference at dawn and dusk, the "active times" of conventional wisdom, was that the deer moved into the open to feed. When the three whitetails moved toward a mown hayfield late in the afternoon, they walked more directly, stopping to nibble only a couple of times. They had already moved fairly close to that field during the day, each bedding area closer to the evening meal.

This fawn is probably eating forbs and grasses at this age, but will continue to nurse until August.

The whitetails' feed and rest cycles ranged from an hour to two-and-a-half hours in length. The routine varied little, and it was obvious that the patterns of undisturbed deer revolved around eating and digesting, with constant vigilance. I won't be redundant, even though the deer were. Whitetails apparently love their routine, so almost anything interesting (from a human observer's perspective) would, by definition, be a disturbance. There were only three interruptions during this 24-hour period.

1:17 pm: D, F&F were bedded and chewing during their fourth rest period of the day. Suddenly the male fawn, who was 50 feet to the east of the others, raised its head erect, ears and eyes focused toward the northeast, directly into the wind. The fawn pulled its head back and snapped it forward like a woodpecker, still rigid. D and the other fawn noticed and focused on the same spot.

Male F suddenly snorted, still lying down. D rose and looked ready for flight at first. She took three stomp-steps toward the object of her interest and stopped. A gray flicker of movement materialized into a coyote, moving steadily south. It passed about 20 yards from the doe and still-bedded fawns, glancing twice in their direction without slowing. D stomped one more time for emphasis as the coyote came by. It kept moving and disappeared over the next hill.

Besides the obvious sanitation benefits, grooming establishes a bond between family members.

With their enthusiasm for nursing, fawns as mature as these will sometimes
lift the doe's hindquarters completely off the ground.

3:36 pm: D and Company were nibbling aster leaves from the forest floor when D went into full alert, this time looking to the southeast. It didn't take me long to spot the intruders. They were talking and snapping brush, tying orange plastic flagging to selected trees. Considering the species of the potential predators, I expected panic. D's next move really surprised me. She walked toward the two foresters, very quietly, until she was 30 yards away. She stood motionless behind a tree as they walked by, talking about last fall's deer hunt.

F&F were still standing about 50 yards farther away, also motionless. Nobody panicked, nobody sneaked away—something I have seen whitetails do hundreds of times. Instead, they were unalarmed and curious. I would make a calculated guess that if it were hunters sneaking along, these three deer would have been gone before I realized any other humans were nearby. The sophistication of a whitetail's perception is underestimated most of the time. They just know.

4:41 pm: D and Company were bedded again, this time near a five-year-old clear-cut with human-tall aspens. D quit chewing and looked along the edge of the clear-cut, south and downwind. The fawns began to look in that direction too. None of the deer looked terribly excited. They would chew for a while and then stop to look in that direction, then look away and chew some more. This went on for almost 10 minutes. By their reaction, I was guessing that other deer were nearby. I finally heard footsteps and then picked up the slight motion of two animals through the underbrush. I was right—two yearling does were approaching D, F&F, eating as they ambled north. The three deer I was hanging out with seemed mostly unconcerned. D was looking away from the new deer, who were now 15 yards away, when her ears went flat against her neck and her back hairs stood up. The closest yearling saw her reaction, stopped, and looked at her. Then it began to nibble again on aspen leaves.

D rose, ears still flat, and took two steps at a right angle from the approaching yearlings. Fair and obvious warning. They stood still, and she ran at them hard. The closest one was too slow as she flicked her left front hoof and hit it on the neck. The yearlings were now in full flight, tails flattened against their rumps in the classic submissive position. They ran in two tight circles and finally off across the clear-cut, trying to shed D in the thick saplings. I heard them crashing through the woods on the other side of the clear-cut and then it was silent. Ten minutes later, D returned, nibbled a bit and lay down by her fawns.

Research suggests that those yearlings will not come back into the area of the encounter for weeks, if at all. Summer feeding ranges are sacred, so it would seem, and hell hath no fury like a dominant doe.

About a half-hour before sunset, D and fawns were in the mown alfalfa field. They fed and bedded four more cycles through the moonlit night, never leaving the field. Night works as cover, just like the woods. I dozed off once, sitting with my back against a huge five-foot diameter bale. I'm not sure how long I was asleep. I snorted myself awake with a start, dreaming about carnivorous sugarplums or something. D was 15 feet away, staring at me. Are you watching us or what?

"I won't let it happen again," I said quietly. She turned and moved slowly away from me. They just know.

After bedding, most deer stretch to loosen their running muscles.

Chapter Five

THE YEAR OF THE DEER

Like most of us animal-types, the whitetail is a creature of the rhythms dictated by nature. These rhythms span lifetimes, generations, and single heartbeats, but the most obvious cycle is represented by the calendar. We chop the wood, put plastic on the windows, do the spring cleaning, or get out the swimsuits, depending on the season. Deer have their equivalent adjustments, eating and layering fat, growing hollow hairs for insulation, returning to their warmer-weather haunts, and molting back to a rusty summer coat. Just being alive, of course, is a solid testament to every creature's abilities to "go with the flow."

In walking us through the year of the whitetail, I am going to concentrate on deer in the far north. The seasons are more pronounced and extreme there, and the whitetail's ability to adapt to those extremes is indicative of its true capacities. Most of the calendar events discussed here happen later in the south (up to two months later in the warmest climates).

These young bucks are a couple of years away from serious sparring, but as with most species, play is practice for later.

The thick winter coat of this post-rut buck hides its thin body. Bucks can lose a quarter of their body weight during the rut.

At this time of year, available browse is less important to survival than the fat reserves of young deer. Deep snow will exaggerate the difficulty of finding food.

I'm not saying that deer farther south are wimp deer—they still get hunted and run over and chased almost constantly. I just think deer in the north might qualify for special status. In an already hard world, theirs is like granite. They live in incredibly harsh climates and are hunted and eaten by darn rear everybody big enough to dream of venison. Life is hard—and then winter comes.

JANUARY

In January, the physiological state of the deer has been called "walking hibernation." Despite appearances—they run at summer speeds when necessary—deer are half as active in the midwinter, eating a third less food. Their metabolism actually drops, in contrast to the way most mammals deal with the cold—by firing up the internal furnace to stay warm.

Whitetails resolutely refuse to budge from the well-packed trails of the "yard," the wintering area. Concentrated numbers of deer translate to better predator detection—many eyes and ears in one place—and the corollary, extra stress.

This stress is usually heaviest on the yard itself. Over-browsing is the rule in northern cedar swamps and western river bottoms, where there is usually no vegetation below the height of a deer standing on its hind legs. The line of flat-bottomed cedars caused by this degree of browsing is visible from a half mile away and is called a "browse line." Obviously, the benefits of yarding outweigh the costs, or whitetails, ever the pragmatists, wouldn't do it.

One factor tipping the scales in favor of an individual deer is its fat reserve . Autumn fat is more important than winter food in the whitetail's survival scheme. In winter, they are going to "starve"

Deer move single-file through their yarding area, creating trails for easier travel.

even with full bellies. Summer foods are 70 percent digestible material, while winter browse is only 10 percent. Under these conditions, eating is not critical. Even artificially well-fed deer lose 15 percent of their autumn weight during the winter. Lower heart rates, lower breathing rates and lower metabolism help conserve some energy. The big difference is that the whitetail's entire digestive chemistry is tuned to fat assimilation. Browsing is almost recreational—it's like they do it just to stay in practice. Make no mistake, lots of deer will die of malnutrition, but the length and intensity of the winter is what kills them. Food availability is not nearly as important.

The "where to hang out" questions tend to have critical consequences. Beds are chosen carefully to reduce heat loss. Deer in snow country have a habit that appears to be counterproductive. They paw away the snow before they lie down, which reduces the insulation under themselves. Some evolutionary scientists think that this behavior indicates deer are new to snow country and have not yet completely adapted to the northern environment.

Deep snow is tough to travel through, even if you have 16-to 24-inch legs, but it makes good insulation. Whitetails actually let themselves be buried during a two-or three-day snowstorm. Their hollow hair insulates so well that the snow over them doesn't melt. Overhead cover also holds warmth, so deer often bed under snow-loaded evergreens. South slopes turn deer into solar collectors. Windbreaks take the chill out of windchill. In general, deer behavior is a model of the energy-efficient lifestyle. They have to conserve, or they die. Our conservation efforts at home don't have quite the same incentive program.

Because of reduced daylight, testosterone production (and therefore sperm production) decreases after December's supplemental, second-chance phase of the breeding season. The changes in body chemistry mean that most bucks toss their antlers, like extra baggage, in January. Some lose antlers earlier or later, with larger bucks, more northerly bucks, and poorly-fed bucks losing them earlier, in general.

Since bucks are, biologically speaking, more expendable than does, nature takes a higher toll on them. A buck's metabolism is higher year-round, and the rut activities can cost them a quarter of their weight before the winter even starts.

FEBRUARY

By February, whitetails compete with each other more directly for food. Constant strife over the limited supply would be counter-productive to

During severe winters, food gets increasingly hard to find.

the energy balance sheet, and deer, of course, have a way to parcel the debits. Equality is a human concept, an ideal, however unworkable it may be. Deer make no pretense. A strict social caste system says dominant bucks eat first, prime does second, then older does, yearlings and fawns. Death begins its persistent gnawing at the tail of this order, most expendable to least. The hierarchy often has does chasing their own fawns from a food source, hardly self-sacrificial behavior.

Aggression progresses in stages, giving the underling plenty of opportunity to back off. First, the ears of the "boss" go straight back, then hackles rise, a wheezing snort further warns the perpetrator, and "slapping" (with front hooves), chasing, and rearing follow. Submission, shown by avoiding eye contact and holding ears back and up, breaks off the contest. Matriarchal does often are dominant over large bucks in these situations, especially if the buck's testosterone levels have lowered and his antlers have been shed. We all know that Mom's the boss.

Starvation alone kills few whitetails—it only sets the stage. Nutrition is the critical element in survival equations. If a deer is malnourished, death can assume a staggering array of shapes. Internal parasites such as stomach worms, flukes, tapeworms, and roundworms, usually no

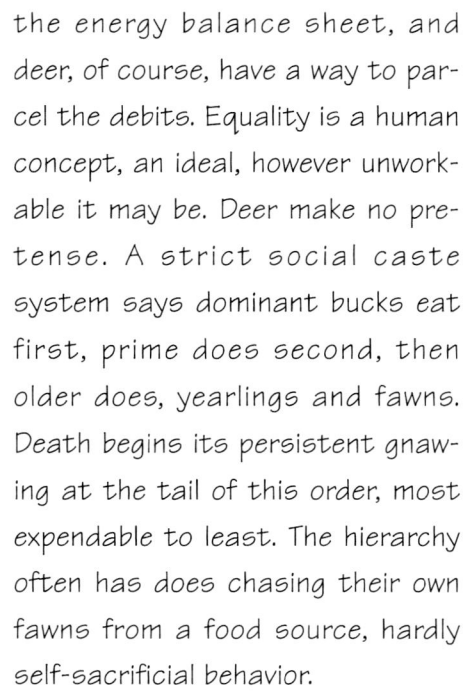

Mature bucks are the first to shed their antlers when winter begins. This buck will lose his shortly.

Whitetails thrive from Mexico to Canada. The deers' adaptability to harsh conditions is legendary.

more than nuisances, can gang up on a starving deer. Deer with expended fat reserves have almost liquid bone marrow and develop nutrition-related diseases like "lumpy-jaw," which affects their ability to eat. Frail whitetails are easier prey—wolves take a large share of rut-weakened bucks, coyotes test fawns with sudden rushes, and cougars pounce on the infirm. But the big share of winter predator kills belongs to Fido, Rover, and Spot. Domestic dogs (more than feral) run down deer for the chase. Dog owners resist the idea that well-behaved pets can revert to their ancestry when no one pulls on the leash. Believe it. Only autos and hunters kill more deer.

MARCH

Prey species. The words suggest something born to be food. True, lots of deer die in March, but dwelling on the ones who don't make it minimizes the fantastic skills of the ones who do. Every meat eater, including the one with the magic to kill from great distances with a rifle, covets the taste of venison. Yet there are far more deer today than a hundred years ago. No other tribute seems necessary.

Day length (photoperiod) pushes deer back to a normal metabolism in mid-March. Bucks tend to be solitary in the early spring. From here on, the length of the remaining winter will be critical. Snow crust conditions determine whether predators will run on top of the snow or punch through. Deer always punch through crusty snow and can be at a fatal disadvantage to wolves, coyotes, and dogs.

Fawns are the tribute that a severe winter demands. Seventy percent is normal mortality in last year's fawns, but it doesn't stop there. An overlooked effect of a long winter is its impact on this year's fawns. In those years, pregnant does

Snow also insulates, so a good bedding area choice includes unpacked snow.

Adolescent bucks tend to gather in small herds during the summer. Groups of "the boys" enjoy social company and have more ears, eyes, and noses for protection.

drop an inordinate number of stillborn fawns or premature fawns that don't survive their first week.

Even social stress, from winter crowding around limited food, has measurable effects. If winter deer densities top 100 deer per square mile, fewer female fawns are born, newborn mortality is high, body size of fawns is smaller, and yearling bucks have diminutive antlers. Ghettos are hard on deer, too.

APRIL

Time to move. Whitetail social groups re-form into two kinds of mini-herds, the matriarchy, a dominant doe and her female offspring, and "the boys," a loose group of two to six males older than two years. They then head for their summer range, which can be as much as 40 miles from the winter yard. If deer are at the end of their metabolic rope in April, any capricious return of winter weather is especially fatal. This is a time when even newly available food may not help. Deer may be too far gone to digest it.

Forest openings are especially important now. Spring sunlight melts snow faster in these small amphitheaters, and the first grasses and forbs push through the mat impatiently. Whitetails can now graze on green instead of browse on brown, and they usually make this transition just in time. They have an uncanny ability to find the forbs with the highest protein levels, and eat those first. In fact, this quest for protein can drive deer to eat some unusual things. There are well documented cases of deer catching and eating fish in shallow streams and digging down into nests of grubs and lady beetles to munch on a protein supplement. In the natural world, there are few 100 percent herbivores (strict plant eaters)—most critters can become omnivorous, eating an animal supplement when the

opportunity presents itself.

Bucks begin new antler growth in April. Velvet nubs on their heads conceal a rapidly developing system of blood vessels and nerves which will, in some cases, branch into one of nature's most regal spectacles.

MAY

Given good nutrition, buck antlers can grow at an astounding rate of a half inch per day. Male hormone (testosterone) levels are still low, making bucks passive "Type B" personalities, for now. It's a good thing. Antlers are delicate and sensitive, mostly blood and nerves, and semi-armed combat now would be messy and painful. Bucks seem to have an uncanny ability to know just how far their antlers spread relative to an upcoming gap in the trees—at the end of the summer very few antlers will be damaged.

In the north, the first fawns are born in late May. They need a head start, for next winter comes early in latitudes above 45 degrees.

Early antler growth in the spring (note the half-winter, half-summer coat) and . . .

An older, larger fawn has the best chance to outlast the long season of snow and cold.

Some yearling does are also pregnant, but they came into estrus a month late the previous fall, so they will drop their fawns in late June. They have single fawns, not twins and triplets like the older does. Only a mild first winter offers these fawns hope of survival. Those born at four pounds have

. . . late summer antlers.

Fawns are led to various hiding places and fed two to five times each day.

little chance; healthy fawns usually weigh eight. In general, the average number of fawns born per doe is slightly over one.

JUNE

Pregnant females isolate themselves, setting up a birthing territory of 10 to 20 acres, usually a traditional area for older does. Subordinate (younger) does must use fringe areas, usually with poorer cover. One population control method for deer is the number of available nurseries.

Depending on the doe's condition, twins are the norm for most prime-age females (but singles or triplets aren't unusual). Fawns usually emerge 15 minutes apart and can walk 20 minutes later. Mom meticulously cleans the birth site, eating placenta, umbilical cord, and all the fluid-stained leaves on the forest floor. Scent control is critical at this vulnerable time.

Soon, the fawns are led to hiding places a few hundred feet apart, and mom comes back only to nurse them two to five times a day, lick their anuses (potty training), and rescue them from danger. Eight ounces of milk is an average meal. Mom and kids "imprint" on each other, mostly by smell, in the first few hours.

Fawns are moved often (to minimize scent) within the nursery area, and the fawns learn to stay within this zone for rescue when predators threaten. The "freezing" behavior of fawns is an automatic shutdown of metabolism called "alarm brachicardia."

Undergrowth makes it harder for sight-feeding coyotes to find fawns, but a lack of thick brush can raise coyote kill rates as high as 80 percent of all fawns. Mom's response to a hungry coyote is more aggressive than you might think. Her melodramatic

"broken wing" routines and out-right attacks belie the normally shy nature of a whitetail.

JULY

Summertime, and the livin' is, well, tolerable, compared to the rest of the year. Deer don't sweat, so they must pant with an exposed tongue to regulate summer heat. Since they don't sweat, whitetails do not need salt and minerals from mineral licks. They apparently just like it. It is sometimes difficult for us humans to see "lower" creatures as having options or doing anything whimsical. The idea that other animals must have some base biological purpose for their actions is less a scientific axiom, in my opinion, than it is a human ego problem.

Whitetail parasites also appreciate the warmth of the summer. Mosquitoes, blackflies, horseflies and, of course, deer flies take their turns at a deer's eyelids, nose, and ears. Usually it's a standoff, with a few flies getting the critical blood meal and producing the trillions of eggs for next year's little lovelies. Deer seem to be prone to liver flukes, which look much worse than they act, at least for a healthy deer. Most deer also carry a parasite called a brainworm, which sounds like something from a science fiction story. Whitetails are resistant to this critter, but other members of their family, like moose and caribou,

Leaves are difficult to convert to winter fat, so whitetails eat almost constantly during the summer months.

The slender look of summer is due to the deer's short-haired coat. Under the thick, hollow winter hair, there is still a deer without much external body fat.

are not. Since deer carry the worm, the problem arises in the northern part of the whitetail's range, where the ranges of deer and moose overlap. Brainworm is primarily responsible for those unusual cases of moose who wander into cities or across prairie farmlands. Those moose usually have advanced brainworm illness at that point and are not long for this world.

Whitetails are infested with ticks during the summer, which, in bad years can cause them to actually rub the hair from their bodies by scratching against trees. If this happens after the winter coat is grown in the fall, it will probably be fatal when the windchills arrive. Deer do get a bum rap regarding Lyme disease. The tiny tick that is the culprit in this case is called the "deer tick." The Lyme tick does feed on deer, but is much more likely to be found on deer mice. It is really the "mouse tick."

Fawns double their weight every two weeks and begin solid food when they are only two weeks old, an age at which they can already outrun a steroid-enhanced human. Theirs is a crash course in adulthood—some are weaned at 10 weeks.

To cope with fawn energy demands, females eat 70 percent of the time during the nursing weeks. Growing fawns bed down often, sleeping only a few minutes, and never staying in one place more than two hours. Older, experienced does move their fawns farther between beds, space litter mates at greater distances, and respond more quickly to danger. This translates to a three to four times better predation survival rate for their fawns than for those of less experienced mothers.

At 25 days, fawns begin to bed together, and when they reach four to six weeks of age, adjacent nursery areas are beginning to disintegrate and overlap. Mom no longer needs to watch them as carefully.

The white spot a few inches up from the rear hoof is the metatarsal gland. Its use to deer is still a mystery.

The "boys," meanwhile, are hanging out, growing status symbols (antlers) and stabilizing their social pecking-order. By late July, antlers are full-sized, biggest on the four- to eight-year-olds. Antler growth is regulated by a complex recipe of food, soil type, age, buck population density, and genetics. Among hundreds of mysteries about deer, one of the most enigmatic is "contralateral" antler growth; if a buck is injured on his right side, the left antler will be stunted.

AUGUST

Food is again getting harder to find, and "rank" is therefore more important. Female dominance is mostly hereditary—grandma rules mom, who rules junior, etc. Males must duel it out on the jousting court. Here, physical size governs. Once the order is established, however, bucks don't waste more energy challenging the acknowledged lords of the woods.

This late summer time is fairly routine. Eat, eat, eat, and sleep. The seasonal changes ripen fruit and nuts, which are available for only short times. Deer make the daily adjustments without missing a beat. Their noses are too good to miss anything, and the genetic program is powerful. They are classic opportunists to whom situation ethics is the norm.

Bucks start to show off their wares (antlers)

The left antler on this deer is malformed either because of a direct injury to the antler during growth or because the deer was injured on the opposite side of its body. The term for the latter condition is "contralateral growth."

A good example of symmetrical antler growth . . .

A dominant buck will often rub quite large trees.

to the does on common feeding grounds, and by late August, shorter days have jump-started testosterone production, mineralizing their antlers. Now begins three months of nonstop action.

SEPTEMBER

Antler velvet is shed in a day, and not by rubbing antlers on small trees, as was commonly thought.

Rubs are mostly done by dominant bucks as a calling card to other bucks—they deposit scent from forehead glands at the same time bark is removed from the tree for a visual signpost. As testosterone levels increase, bucks rub trees more and more, releasing pent-up energy and scent-marking with their forehead glands.

One-and-a-half-year-old males are now driven out of the matriarchal group. Because of the new restlessness brought on by their first experience with testosterone, they may travel 20 miles away, a dispersal distance that effectively prevents inbreeding. To everything there is a purpose, especially when survival is the subject.

In openings, bucks begin to spar half-heartedly, but only among their social group. Dominant bucks begin to make scrapes. Rub-trails mark the normal travel routes of these boss bucks, who are just beginning to get warmed up.

The pre-rut time is strictly photoperiod-controlled in the north, to accurately time breeding and the birth of fawns. Southern whitetails have the luxury of less weather pressure and respond with a mint julep approach to breeding—don't hurry, be happy. In general, the breeding season moves to a later date as we watch deer farther south, but there is a wrinkle in that generalization—literally and figuratively. Whitetails in the middle states, like Missouri, Tennessee, and Kentucky, among others,

breed slightly earlier than northern deer. Some scientists think the survival strategy at work here is that does can afford to have fawns earlier because of the earlier spring, so they do. That ensures that the fawns are older, larger, and more fit when the winter comes again.

OCTOBER

Bucks are now getting a taste of hormone overload. Dominant males, mostly nocturnal and solitary, become aggressive. Real push-fights rarely happen within fraternal groups, but on the edges of home ranges, rival dominants may meet. Rule 1: there is only one boss deer. The combatants snort-wheeze, a rapid inhale-exhale which says, "Your mother wears army hooves." They then walk sideways toward each other with their ears back, aim at each other about 15 feet away and the fight is on. It lasts until there is a winner.

By the time bucks reach their eighth year, they are challenged often and use too much critical energy responding. The odds against a buck reaching 10 years? A quarter-million to one.

Buck home ranges grow to three square miles or more. At certain check-points in their travels, usually at the intersections of doe trails, they begin scraping in earnest. The primary requirement for a scrape location is an overhanging branch

The winner in this duel will enjoy a priority mating status.

The last traces of velvet are sometimes removed by antler rubbing, but rubbing is usually done for another purpose, and the velvet is removed incidentally.

This buck prepares a scrape below a scenting branch by pawing away the ground vegetation. Scent-marking will follow.

about four feet high. Nibbling on the branch, boss buck leaves saliva (Brut), and sebaceous gland scent from his nose (English Leather). Between his divided hooves is interdigital scent (Old Spice), which is left by the scraping action. Then he hunches up and urinates (Aqua Velva) over the tarsal glands on his rear legs (Jovan) and into the scrape. What doe could possibly resist such an arsenal? At the very least, she will hang around a while, and that's what the buck is counting on.

Scraping activity peaks at the end of this month and helps deer size up prospects for the coming breeding season.

NOVEMBER

Experienced does come into estrus first, in early November, and bucks are chasing them all month. "Tending grunts" stimulate females to urinate so males can check their condition. Checking is done with a lick of the doe's personal areas, smelling the tarsal glands, and the lip-curl called the "flehmen" posture. Boss bucks are active during the day for the first time all year, and the significance of that change is not lost on hunters. In fact, bucks are so active they can lose 25 percent of their body weight in the breeding season. The things we do for love . . .

Does increase their activity level the day before estrus, insuring that their random wanderings will

This doe is urinating. The pursuing buck will smell the spot to determine her receptivity.

Sparring matches seldom last for more than a few seconds, but if the
bucks are closely matched in size and aggressiveness, bucks will literally exhaust themselves.

catch the attention of a buck. Scrapes are all but abandoned by now.

In the north, breeding during this first estrus (does can have another estrus 28 days later if they remain unbred) is important for fawn development. Eighty to ninety percent of mature does breed in just a few days in November. It peaks on the 10th. Intense activity is the rule.

The "act" itself is anticlimactic, by human standards. The buck mounts the receptive doe from the rear, thrusts two or three times, and it's over. From about the 20th of November on, exhausted bucks go into seclusion, resting for the second phase of the rut, in early December.

DECEMBER

December begins the time of reckoning for deer. In the south, the breeding season is just getting started, but northern deer are already winding down their amorous activity. A second estrus, for those does who somehow didn't breed during November, peaks at mid-month. Deer in the far north may not get much of this second chance; here is where winter overlaps even the early estrus.

Ten inches of snow seems to be the critical depth. Schools close, and deer "yard up." These deer yards, concentrated winter gathering areas, are traditional, generation after generation. Young deer learn the routes (sometimes 40 miles) to these yards from the matriarch. Food doesn't seem to be a critical factor in the location of wintering areas, but evergreen cover or some other wind protection does seem to be a common requirement.

Far northern deer locate their yards on the boundaries between wolf pack territories, not by choice, but by default. Deer who attempt to winter over in the middle of wolf territories don't live long enough to breed. The "demilitarized zone" between wolf packs is a buffer area, where wolves avoid inter-pack conflict, and deer take advantage.

A day in the life of a whitetail toward the end of this month goes something like this: At sunrise, travel a mile to the feeding area, eat breakfast, then bed down; lunch at noon, bed down; dinner at sunset, bed down for the longest rest of the day one hour after sunset; get up twice for midnight snacks. Sounds boring, right? For a deer, whose stressful life is often on the razor edge of death, boring translates to another day of breathing.

"Stress" is relative. Deer define the word stress far more graphically than we do. But the greatest tribute to their nearly magical abilities is that, next spring, in a favorite woods, we will once again see trails, scats, browse, and beds along the footpath. Perhaps someday we will be properly impressed.

Travel through deep snow uses critical calories. "Yarding up" and creating a network of packed trails is essential for whitetail survival.

Chapter Six
DEER LORE

I had need.
I have dispossessed you of beauty,
    grace, and life.
I have taken your spirit from its
    worldly frame.
No more will you run in freedom
Because of my need

I had need.
You have in life served your kind
    in goodness.
By your life, I will serve my brothers
    and sisters.
Without you I hunger and
    grow weak.
Without you I am helpless, nothing.

I had need.
Give me your flesh for strength.
Give me your covering for
    protection.
Give me your bones for my labors.
And I shall not want.

— Ojibwe Prayer to a Slain Deer

The Anishnabe, or Ojibwe, people of the northern forests watched animals carefully. Their lives depended on the knowledge they gained from their observations. Most animals were endowed with certain traits of character, and the Anishnabe tried to imitate the behaviors they admired, to form themselves in the image of those ideals. Note that the frame of reference for desired behavior was not the human animal. Humans were not thought to innately possess any of those desired traits—they were learned behaviors. In this way the Ojibwe did not learn about animals, in the scientific sense, but learned from them how to live. There was no assumption, as in western society, that the animals were somehow inferior. There were human people, bear people, tree people, rock people—all equally gifted with their own views of the world. They all reflected the future, fed each other, and taught each other.

The level of respect given to the rest of nature by aboriginal humans on every continent showed this same wisdom. Without any fossil record to guide them, there was still the correct assumption that the other "people" were our elders and they should have the same respect as human elders, if not more. Success, in this case measured by the longevity of the species, was not open to argument. An hierarchy of "importance" had to be manufactured by western civilization and drawn in biology books with humans at the apex of the evolutionary tree. The First Peoples on our continent had no such illusions.

This misguided idea of separateness from nature led western civilization, at least at first, to kill far more of nature than necessary—nothing should stand in the way of the "progress" of the human species. We have an environmental

nightmare to show for it.

Today, we have a movement in reaction to that land-hungry way of thinking that assumes that life is sacred. Don't kill anything. Traditional peoples would agree, in part. But, thinking only as far back as breakfast, they would also remind us that death is sacred too, as is soil formation from dead bodies, killing, eating, defecating, and all of the other processes of the universe. No matter what our philosophical point of departure, we white European types stubbornly refuse to look through a wide-angle lens.

The assumption of Native peoples, a logical one from a perspective of equality, was that all beings deserved life. This led to a paradox, especially concerning the white-tailed deer. In order for humans to live, some deer had to die.

If there is a recurring theme in Native American stories about deer, it is one of reconciliation of this paradox. If animals were ever taken for granted, they would be justifiably insulted and refuse to give themselves to humans thereafter. The subtle message here is that deer make choices too. Instead of the human-centered view that "I can't hunt very well," there is a humble acknowledgment that the world has its own plan independent of our wishes. An unsuccessful hunter would more likely say "Deer don't want to die for me today."

One story from the Ojibwe is quite blunt about the human responsibility to be humble. The deer had vanished from the land of the Anishnabe, and the humans roamed over the world in search of them. Owl, who often foretells things to come, found all the deer in a huge corral far to the north. They grazed and browsed as if nothing at all were wrong. The curious owl flew down to question the deer, but a flock of crows attacked the owl and drove it away. The owl escaped their beaks only because it was night, and it could see and hear better than the crows.

When the owl reported the location of the deer, the humans formed a large war party to rescue them. Owl guided them back to the gates of the enclosure, but they were surprised by an attack of the fierce crows. The battle lasted for days, but no side gained an advantage. The deer made no attempt to escape—they just watched.

Finally the chief of the humans asked for a truce, realizing that defeating the crows would cost as much in human suffering as in crow suffering. The crows laughed that humans could only learn this lesson the hard way.

Then the chief of the Anishnabe asked the deer why they were so unconcerned about the rescue attempt, especially since the war party had suffered so much. The deer chief answered that they

were in this place by choice—the crows had treated them much better than humans ever had. Humans had wasted their flesh, spoiled their lands, and desecrated their bones. The two-leggeds had dishonored the deer and therefore themselves. "Without you we can live very well, but without us you will die."

The Anishnabe promised to stop offending the lives, deaths, and spirits of the deer, and the deer followed the humans back to their lands. Today, they honor this as the oldest and most sacred treaty. It is unthinkable to forget where life originates—from the deer's gift of itself.

The Wintu people of Northern California believed that the successful taking of a deer had a prerequisite level of skill, preparation, and respect, but the crucial element was the choice made by the deer. If any part of the human responsibility—not wasting, humility, gratitude, courtesy—is forgotten, the deer will "forget" to show up next time.

The Cherokee believed that this level of respect had direct positive effects on individuals and direct negative effects if the rites were not done in sincerity. A long time ago, humans and deer lived in peace. Humans hunted and killed deer only when they needed food and clothing. Then something happened to change it all—they invented bows and arrows. Humans could now kill at great distance, effortlessly. They began to kill unnecessarily, and the animals were afraid they would be eradicated. They had a meeting. The bears made bows even stronger than the human bows, but their claws were too long to shoot the bows. When they removed their claws they could not climb trees. The bears decided against such a compromise.

The other animals met in their groups and attempted to find a way to fight the humans, but they had as much success as the bears. The last group to meet was the deer, whose leader was Awi Udsi, Little Deer. They realized there was no way to stop the humans from killing, but there might be a way to change the way they killed. Awi Udsi went to the humans in their sleep and told them that they must prepare for the hunt with rituals. They must ask permission to take a deer. They must ask for pardon from the deer's spirit after the kill. If they did not do all of these things, the meat from the deer would make them sick and crippled. Deer did have control of the quality of their meat.

A few hunters didn't believe that Awi Udsi was anything more than a dream and soon became crippled and sick. Those who understood the dream lesson, that everything is dependent on everything else, never took the presence of deer for granted and never wanted for deer to eat.

Compared to bears, wolves, coyotes, spiders, eagles, hawks, bison, and a number of other animals, deer aren't mentioned as often in Native lore. Considering their importance to human survival, this is somewhat surprising. It is entirely possible that including white-tailed deer as characters in stories would be a risk—if the character were somehow offensive to the deer, the deer could withhold their flesh from human consumption. It would always be foolish to gamble with the whitetail's gracious gift of itself. Being discrete about deer is good politics.

There is, perhaps, another reason why deer are scarce in Native lore. The deer hunters I know (at least the ones I respect) always feel some guilt when they take the life of a whitetail. Humans have a natural avoidance of uncomfortable topics, and it is difficult to explain the paradox a hunter feels between respect and admiration for a living deer

always conditions). Toward the end of one story, after he has unsuccessfully tried to be a beautiful but flightless bird and an arrow who flies high but always comes down, Iktomi sees some playing fawns and begins to covet their beautiful brown and white spots.

"How did you get those wonderful spots?" he asks. A fawn looked at Iktomi carefully, and answered that its mother marked its face with coals from a red hot fire. "'She dug a hole in the ground for me and made a soft bed of grass and twigs in it. Then she covered me with sweet grass and dry cedars. From a fire she borrowed a large red ember and tucked it next to my face to make the spots."

"Will you do the same for me?" Iktomi asked, still trying to be someone other than himself. The fawn agreed to do it, trying to keep a straight face.

and the good taste of venison. When you can't explain it, don't. If the wonderful attributes of the white-tailed deer were celebrated too much, it could make the necessary duties of survival much more difficult.

There is also a chance that the deer may get revenge someday, as happens in a tale about Iktomi, the snare-weaver, a sometimes-human-sometimes-spider character of the Lakota people. Iktomi is part young, naive bumbler and part crafty trickster, in the tradition of Coyote in the South and West. He always wants what he doesn't have, but can't seem to observe the conditions under which he is given new attributes (and there are

"Make sure you pile extra grass and cedars on top of me, because I want better spots than you have," Iktomi demanded. The fawn was happy to accommodate. It put the hot coal among the dry grass and scampered away, leaving Iktomi to his self-imposed fate.

Aside from the lesson on being who we are, the message says that deer owe us nothing—we owe them.

Unusual animals of any species were treated conservatively. Often just the fact that an animal was out of the ordinary meant it must be present for a special reason, such as the delivery of a special message. It was best not to take chances, so these animals were seldom killed. Even though ordinary white-tailed deer are infrequently mentioned in Native American lore, these special animals were treated differently. When I was a kid, I heard many stories about Native people and white buffalo. Albino bison were thought to have great powers, and the same is true of white deer.

The Umpqua people of southern Oregon owe a debt to the white deer. Once, a terrible disease spread through the Umpqua nation, killing hundreds of people. The medicine men and women of the Umpqua went to the top of the nearby Cascade Mountains, somewhere near Crater Lake, to fast and pray. It didn't work, at least at first.

The most beautiful and competent young woman in the largest village, a chief's daughter named Teola, then became sick. No one ever recovered from this dread disease, and so the people were very sad, chanting the death songs or sitting quietly. A white deer came out of the dark forest and walked around the woman's lodge three times, each time looking in the door at Teola. The third time around, this deer walked inside and stretched its neck toward Teola. She reached her hand toward the white deer and touched its nose. Then the deer walked back into the forest. Teola sat up from her bed and was completely healed.

Since that day, the Umpqua people never kill an albino deer for food. Some Umpqua are firm in their belief that the reason white society is so unsettled and environmentally harmful today is that they killed white deer indiscriminately. This showed the Great Mystery that they did not respect the world enough to look for messages from the rest of nature.

The Lakota people of the northern plains believe that white deer are the visible forms of strange people who live out in the wilds, or sometimes the form in which those who have died return to give us important messages. There are many stories of women pleading with hunters to spare a white deer,

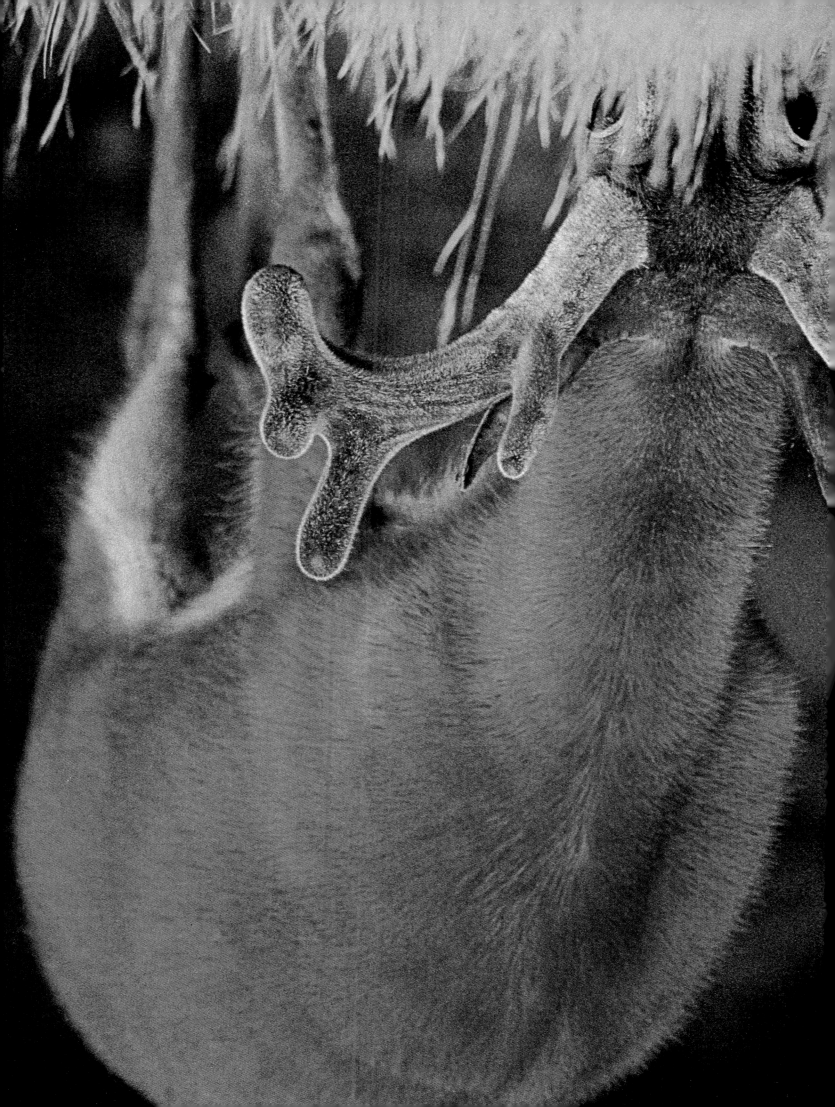

usually because it is a departed relative. The general tempering message from women to men is to use those traditionally masculine powers wisely and listen to the advice of women. Because of the female nurturing power, they will see things that are not obvious to men. These complementary perspectives are essential to a balanced view for all of us.

Perhaps one lesson the deer can bring to us even today is to listen, watch, be patient, and consider irreversible decisions carefully—it is sometimes wise to be a deer.

Chapter Seven
DEER MAGIC

Creation is a mixture of things, including living creatures, the processes that change those creatures through time, and the relationships between those creatures and their processes.

But I think it's also made of stories. I am not sure what motivates me to tell stories about whitetails, but I do know that a good part of my life has been spent in this pursuit. It seems to fit who I am.

Once (upon a time) I was canoeing on one of my favorite Minnesota "sneak" rivers, the Tamarack. Somewhere along the river, a trail too rough to be a beaver or otter slide came down the bank, across the shallows, and up the other bank. A deer trail, heavily used. This was a paddling day, with miles to go before I slept, but the trail still caught my natural Odocoilean curiosity. I climbed the bank and peeked over the edge. I saw 10 ears pointed in different directions. The math said five deer, all still unaware of me. I eased my head up a few inches farther. They were lying down, calmly chewing their cuds. So complete was their disbelief when they saw me that they assumed (it seemed) I was another deer

Whitetails drink only when they need to—it's a vulnerable time for them.

A magic morning graced by a mysterious appearance.

One thing I have noticed is that the whitetail's instinctive programming won't allow it to recognize a predator inside of a critical distance, about 50 feet in most cases. Their defenses are so effective they seem almost arrogant (a deer's version of arrogance, to be sure). The logic probably goes: "How could anyone possibly get that close? And if they are that close, they must not be dangerous, or we would be dead by now."

This "critical distance" factor has led to some other memorable experiences. Once, in the East Texas swamp country, I was perched eight feet up in an oak. It was a sticky late summer day and I had no hope of being scentless, as I was dripping onto the leaves below. A small forkhorn buck had approached within a few

These two traveling companions have either already decided dominance or they will shortly.

and had been there all along. They looked away from me, alert for real danger. Intruders certainly wouldn't come out of the river. . .

If deer wore pants, the belt would have been down around their metatarsal glands.

On this day, the deer—the closest one only four feet from my face—were now double-taking, incredulous, wondering why this deer had such small ears and nose, and why it smelled . . . like . . . a . . . two-legged. Two-legged? They actually spun out in the leaves, and in three seconds there were only five warm ovals on the ground to show for my experience. I was the manifestation of their worst nightmare and probably the subject of future deer folklore.

yards of me, casually nibbling at random leaves and mushrooms. I was still for 15 minutes, wondering why my scent hadn't invoked a hair-up panic.

I decided to experiment. "Hi, deer," I said at a normal conversational volume. Before I had finished the last consonant, eyes and ears were aimed on me—that typical intense stare I had seen so many times when I hadn't invited it. I waved. The deer bobbed its head, tense and ready. "If I were a cougar you would be missing some pieces right now," I said. It still didn't move. I shifted to another position in the tree. To my surprise, the deer flipped its tail once and simply resumed feeding. "You are not a cougar because I am missing no parts," it seemed to say with its nonchalance.

I had a 20-minute conversation with this deer. I did most of the talking. It listened by flipping its ear in my direction every time I started a new discourse. When I finally moved down the tree, the deer skipped a few paces farther away and started feeding again, checking my noises with its closest ear. It was barely concerned. I was slightly insulted because I had always considered myself a little more intimidating.

This whitetail wasn't shocked that I had penetrated its defense system—it had simply decided that anything so nearby that hadn't acted in a threatening manner was no threat. It was, of course, correct.

Now that I've explained these behaviors rationally, isolating the variables and assuming the most plausible explanation, I'll confess something else to you. I don't believe the rational explanation is the entire explanation. I think that sometimes whitetails just know. It's true that a case can be made for the unexplainable being only as yet unexplained. And, perhaps as early as next week many ESP-ish phenomena will be thoroughly elucidated by some as-yet unrecognized external cue. Until then, I will stubbornly attribute the following events of a day in Wyoming's North Platte River bottoms to "magic."

I was walking a deer path on the slope above the river flats, in the open. Below, the trees were spaced wide enough to allow small patches of sunlight to

Dominant, older, smarter does travel first in line . . .

reach the forest floor. I was lost in my thoughts as I walked, but then I interrupted myself. "I should be watching for deer." I have often done this interruption process with bear and other animals, and too often for pure coincidence, I looked up to see the bear, coyote, or whatever. I don't think there is anything particularly magical about this "sensing" of an animal presence nearby—they usually have strong smells, and even though my brain can not consciously decipher the odor into an "I smell bear" message, I associate something with bears.

The whitetails were there, of course. Three velvet-antlered bucks were lying 50 yards below in one of the sunlit patches, eyes riveted on me. They had

that ready-to-flee look, and I expected them to do just that. The sunlight must have had the same narcotic effect on them as it had on me. I didn't move and they didn't either. I sat down slowly on a rock and watched.

For the first few minutes they were ready to bolt. I had already been discovered, so, again, I began to talk to them in a relaxed voice. It took a few more minutes before they began to unwind their coiled springs a little, and they ignored me more and more. I stood up. (Full alert again.) I talked. (They relaxed.) I walked slowly, talking as I went, at an angle that brought me a little closer. (Alert.) I was careful not to walk directly at them. I stopped. (They relaxed again.)

Over the course of two hours I zig-zagged in this pattern, conversing. By that time I had moved within 10 feet of the closest deer. They watched intently as I lay down in the stiff grass and began to "browse" with my hand. At that point they decided, despite the awful human smell, that I should earn my keep if I was going to lay down in their company. On cue they all turned their heads in other directions, alert for "predators," and ignored me. The implied message was (it seemed), "Get to work. That direction is yours to watch." Weird as it might seem, I took my assigned responsibilities seriously. I watched.

An hour later one of the deer rose and began to feed, moving away from "us." I moved out next, slowly, talking, heart still pounding from what I expect will be the only experience I will ever have at being a deer. I am, to this day, honored.

Another time, in Wisconsin, my encounter took place 20 feet up in an oak tree on the edge of a mown hay field. It was mid-autumn and all the leaves had dropped except for those on that oak.

The perfect hiding spot. A white-tailed doe and almost-grown fawn came into the field and moved slowly to a place 80 feet from the tree. The short green grass was the last they would see before winter, and they fed as though that were the case, looking up for danger less often than usual. The sun was down and it was getting dark. Suddenly they both aimed their eyes and ears to my right, to the far corner of the field. They were statues, not flicking an ear or even chewing the grass in their mouths.

Finally, the reason for their concern appeared in the field. A coyote trotted nonchalantly along the edge of the woods a few hundred feet away from where they stood, moving steadily along the edge. There was a slight difference in the way the doe reacted compared to its fawn. The doe remained rigid, but the fawn began to act more and more skittish as the coyote moved toward them. The fawn looked toward the woods and back at the coyote, then back at the woods. It glanced at the woods more and more often as the coyote moved to within 50 yards. The fawn was telegraphing its intentions, but the doe remained still, seemingly calling the coyote's bluff.

The fawn bolted into the woods, running directly under my tree, and simultaneously the coyote melted into the trees on the same side of the field, but still a hundred feet from my position. Just behind me the woods erupted with the sound of many coyote feet. The fawn ran in a circle. There were yips and growls, a fawn bleat, and it was still—over in seconds. My hair was standing up and I felt that greasy cold feeling, knowing it was dark, and I still had to walk back to the car.

When I looked back to the field, the doe was feeding again, looking occasionally toward the place

In a matter of weeks, these two bucks will not be so friendly.

where its fawn had died. The seemingly callous indifference to the demise of its offspring amazed me, with my human values, but I realized that I can never appreciate the world view of a creature that loses half of its population every year. Emotional attachments and mourning would be a shortcut to extinction. Deer are, only and gloriously, deer. "Who they are" works for them and has for millions of years. Which newly arrived animal, two-legged or otherwise, has the right to question a record that long-standing?

I was asked once about my favorite deer experience. I thought about those I have recounted here, and some others I haven't mentioned. I thought about the amazing tenacity of a creature with such a frail, graceful bearing. I thought about all the times my heart has been in my throat as a deer walked within a few feet of my hiding spots.

"Of all the experiences I have had," I answered, "my favorite one is the next one."

*Three alert deer, one feeding. This is the typical vigilance of the whitetail,
ensuring that at least some survive each year to reproduce—and to grace our lives.*

DEER PEOPLE

LIVING WITH DEER

Stan Stevenson remembers feeding fawns from bottles when he was five years old. He had one bottle in each hand, and the fawns kept nudging the bottles like they would an udder. It was hard to hold the bottles without dropping them, but he did. That was over 50 years ago. Figuratively, he hasn't dropped a bottle since.

Stan owns the "Farm," as he calls it, but the only crop he grows is deer. The Farm is a 50-acre enclosure in northern Wisconsin, and it has been the home of three generations of Stevensons and countless generations of whitetails. Stan went off to Chicago to seek his fortune when he was a young man—he wasn't really enamored with the deer on his parents' farm. He remembers being indifferent about them years later when he and his wife, Esther, moved back to the home place. But they grew on him. And grew . . .

Stan now feeds 40-some deer, 365 days a year, and still gets a kick from watching them come over the hill in a solemn parade. "They are so quiet," he says when asked what in the world the attraction is.

When Stan used to jog, there were deer who couldn't stand to be left out of the fun—they would jog alongside every day. Occasionally, new fawns will be eaten by a bear that breaks into the enclosure, and bucks have killed each other in dominance disputes, but in general, Stan's deer have it pretty cozy. There is an apple orchard that belongs to them. Stan built a special shed just for the thousands of dollars worth of deer food he feeds them every year. It's a good life compared to that of whitetails living outside the fencing.

Stan collects antlers as they are shed each year and has noticed patterns. The oldest bucks lose theirs first, followed by the youngest, the mature dominant bucks, and finally the nearly mature bucks shed in the last part of January. The sequence probably makes some sense. The oldest and youngest bucks have less need for antlers than those in the thick of the dominance struggle. Of the prime bucks, the most dominant use the most breeding energy and probably experience a sharper drop in their testosterone levels after the rut.

The stories Stan remembers most vividly are the fights between his "big boys." Two bucks named Felix and Moose fought steadily for 15 minutes once, until they bled from their nostrils.

The decision? A draw. "Butch" and "Pat" both showed up with bloody antlers at different times. They had apparently gored lesser bucks. Later, Butch mortally wounded Pat in a brawl. Rudy, a huge deer, used to threaten other bucks with sidelong walking while he was still 150 yards away.

Strangely, Stan has never been gored, or even come close. He is careful most of the time, but remembers kneeling more than once to spread corn around and looking up to see huge antlers inches from his face—during the rut. The opportunity has been there, but no deer in 50 years has taken advantage.

The reason is clear to Stan. "They know me. I'm "food" to those deer, not competition. They keep those things separate. They're a lot smarter than we give them credit for."

BUCK FEVER

Ken Nordberg has been in the woods 4,000 hours a year for 15 years, watching deer. As you might conclude, this kind of commitment borders on obsession. In order to keep from being locked up somewhere, Ken had to do two things. One, he had to demonstrate that he wasn't a danger to society, and two, he made watching deer into a full-time paying occupation. About 1980, dentistry had lost its luster for Dr. Nordberg, and he was just mad enough about the misinformation he saw in deer hunting articles to make a career out of setting the record straight. Conventional wisdom about deer may never recover. He is now finishing his seventh edition of the *Whitetail Hunter's Almanac* and has already made a long lifetime's worth of contributions to the body of whitetail knowledge.

Ken's method is simple. He is out there nearly all the time, watching wild deer. "Penned whitetails are another species," Nordberg states flatly. "In fact, the differences in behavior between fawns, yearlings, adult does, lesser bucks, and dominant bucks are significant enough to consider them separately."

He now has six study areas, and he takes copious notes, pausing yearly to organize them into the newest edition of the Almanac. Each edition is loaded with information on track sizes, bed sizes, different stages of the rut, how wolves hunt deer, and constant stories—reminders of the whitetail's incredible ability to learn.

Whitetails go way back in Ken's memory. He remembers looking far up into a tree at deer his dad had killed on their farm in northern Minnesota. He remembers touching the nose of a curious wild fawn that ran right up to him in the woods. Perhaps, at the age of eight, it was some kind of anointment into a life of deer-watching. Maybe the deer chose him . . .

One of his favorite deer was a doe named "Redhead," a deer who learned to accept Ken (and only Ken) as a normal occupant of her woods. For five years she would "present" her new fawns to Ken when he arrived in the late spring on his initial study area. She physically pushed her fawns over to him for inspection. Deer learn and pass that learning on to their offspring. "They get measurably smarter every year," he says, without blinking.

On this plot of land, Ken was around when 18 deer died. Eight were poached, five were crippled, three were taken by unethical methods, and only two were killed by completely legal means. Instead of channeling his anger into hating hunters he set out to educate them about the constant yearly behavioral changes in deer, in the hopes of nurturing some respect and respectful behavior in a typically frustrated hunter.

Wolf-watching has become a new interest, especially regarding their relationships with deer. Ken has watched many packs of wolves move. They check every track for some scent signal that a deer has a weakness. "It's amazing to watch," he says. "They will go 'no, no, no, no, no,' then 'yes,' and proceed to hunt and kill a specific deer. When they don't have their noses down, checking tracks, the deer just ignore them. For that little while, there's a truce, and nobody has to use extra energy."

At a certain point, it would seem that so much first-hand knowledge would dull a sense of wonder. Ken Nordberg hasn't lost his. "Whitetails migrate to their winter yards in one night," he says, scratching his head. "I have looked at all the previously stated reasons, by all the scientists and other observers, and there is no sense to it. They know exactly when to go, and they are not letting us in on it."

I got the feeling he liked it that way.

DR. DEER

Larry Marchinton remembers being out with his family at night on the Florida back roads "looking for eyes." When he was a little kid, using the headlights to find nocturnal wanderers was a favorite family recreation. On this particular night, a fawn had been temporarily blinded by the glare and walked within two feet of Larry's side of the car. Little did Larry's parents suspect that a match had been struck in his belly that would spread into an inferno. Now, at age 55, with 200 scientific publications under his belt, Larry Marchinton admits to being worse off than ever.

"For every answer there are 20 more questions," he says of his research. "And we're just getting to the interesting stuff now."

In fairness, some of the things Marchinton has already done are pretty darned interesting too. He pioneered the use of radio-telemetry on deer and developed the concept of "movement ecology"—where they go for what reasons. He recognized scrapes and rubs as complex communication "sign-posts," and helped develop the idea of scent pheromones as behavior-altering factors among whitetails. He is presently on the verge of proving that mature (four plus years) buck urine has a "priming" effect on the mating behavior of does, through a "vomeronasal organ" in a deer's nasal passages, indicating the importance of mature bucks in effective game management.

The list of accomplishments goes on, to the point where Larry Marchinton, biologist at the University of Georgia School of Forest Resources, is widely recognized as an expert on the behavior of white-tailed deer. He got that title the old-fashioned way, as the saying goes.

"Athens #1," named after his home town these days, was a tame mature buck that allowed Larry and his assistants to follow him around day and night. Does in heat actually took a cue from Athens and were human-tame in his presence. He was a "gold mine," who opened the doors to the concept of sign-posts. Interestingly, during the peak of the rut, Athens would defend his scrapes against Larry and the crew.

Once, when experimenting with the escape behavior of deer, Larry and a trailing hound were on the tracks of a radio-collared doe that had apparently bedded down in a row of slashings in the middle of a clear-cut. Larry, the dog, and an assistant were 15 yards from the radioed deer when a deer jumped and ran away. The dog relieved itself and went off after the deer. Larry did too, but soon realized that the radio signal was coming from behind him. He went back to the pile of brush and stood near where the dog had urinated, crouched down and saw his radio-collared deer three feet from his face, looking back. Only then did the deer make its escape.

These days, Larry describes his respect for the whitetail as "semi-religious." He believes that on the European and North American continents, humans and deer evolved together as inseparable predator and prey. "They made us who we are," he says.

REFERENCES

Atkeson, T. & Marchinton, 1988. Vocalizations of white-tailed deer. *American Midland Naturalist* 120: 194-200

Caduto, M. & Bruchac, 1988. Keepers of the Earth. Fulcrum Press, Colorado.

Caduto, M. & Bruchac, 1991. Keepers of the Animals. Fulcrum Press, Colorado.

Clark, E., 1953. Indian Legends of the Pacific Northwest. University of California Press, Los Angeles, California.

Cox, D. & Ozoga, 1988. Whitetail Country. NorthWord Press, Minocqua, Wisconsin.

Eastman, C., 1909. Wigwam Evenings. University of Nebraska Press, Lincoln, Nebraska.

Eteling, K., 1989. Hunting Superbucks. Sedgewood Press, New York, New York.

Johnston, B., 1976. Ojibway Heritage. University of Nebraska Press, Lincoln, Nebraska.

Marchinton, R.L., 1983. Reproductive behavior in white-tailed deer and related vocalizations. *Quality Deer Management Association, Greenville, South Carolina.*
- 1992. The biology of the rut. *Quality Deer Management Association, Athens, Georgia.*
- 1987. Signposting in whitetails and its sociobiological implications. SW Missouri State University, Springfield, Missouri.
- 1968. Telemetric study of white-tailed deer movement, ecology and ethology in the Southeast. Ph.D. Diss., Auburn University

Morriseau, N., 1965. Legends of my People. Ryerson Press, Toronto, Canada.

Nordberg, K., 1988-93. Whitetail Hunter's Almanac. Editions 1-6, Shingle Creek Press, Minneapolis, Minnesota.

Rogers, L., 1983. Walking with Deer. North Cent. Forest Exper. Station Spec. Pub., St. Paul, Minnesota.

Rue, L., 1978. The Deer of North America. Crown Publishers, New York, New York.

Suzuki, D. & Knudson, 1992. Wisdom of the Elders. Bantam Books, New York, New York.

Wessells, N., Ed., 1968. Vertebrate Adaptations. W.H. Freeman & Co., San Francisco, California.

Whitetails Unlimited, 1993. *The Deer Trail.*, W.U., Sturgeon Bay, Wisconsin.

Zitkala-Sa, 1901. *Old Indian Legends.* University of Nebraska Press, Lincoln, Nebraska.